Undivided

Developing a Worldview Approach to Biblical Integration

Martha E. MacCullough

Purposeful Design Publications is the publishing division of the Association of Christian Schools International (ACSI) and is committed to the ministry of Christian school education, to enable Christian educators and schools worldwide to effectively prepare students for life. As the publisher of textbooks, trade books, and other educational resources within ACSI, Purposeful Design Publications strives to produce biblically sound materials that reflect Christian scholarship and stewardship and that address the identified needs of Christian schools around the world.

The views expressed in this publication are those of the author, and they may not necessarily represent the position of the Association of Christian Schools International.

Unless otherwise identified, all Scripture quotations are taken from the Holy Bible, NEW INTERNATIONAL VERSION®. Copyright © 1973, 1978, 1984, 2011 by Biblica, Inc. All rights reserved worldwide. Used by permission of Biblica, Inc.

Printed in the United States of America

25 24 23   5 6 7

MacCullough, Martha Elizabeth.

    Undivided: developing a worldview approach to biblical integration

    ISBN 978-1-58331-553-8 Catalog #6262

Designer: Mike Riester

Cover Image: Thinkstock.com

Editorial team: Chandler Birch, Frieda Nossaman

Purposeful Design Publications
A Division of ACSI
PO Box 62249 • Colorado Springs, CO 80962
1-800-367-0798 • www.purposefuldesign.com

Contents

To all of my former education students
who are living with an undivided heart for God
and helping students develop a biblical worldview out of which to think and act.

Acknowledgments

When one has lived and served in Christian education for so many years, innumerable people and experiences contribute to growth and development along the way. Worldview thinking and acting has been a passion of mine since I read Francis Schaeffer's first book. But it is the students God allowed me to teach whom I must acknowledge in the writing of this book. They inspired me to study and learn. Because of them, I am passionate about teachers and students developing undivided hearts out of which to think and act in all of life *and* learning.

I acknowledge those who encouraged me to continue developing the model addressed in this book, including ACSI regional directors who provided copies of taped seminars to their area schools and invited me to deliver addresses on the topic at regional and national conferences. It was, however, Dr. Jay Desko who encouraged me to put these ideas into writing in a booklet format, eventually published under the School of Education at Cairn University. This book is an expansion of that first booklet.

I acknowledge and appreciate my gifted editor, Chandler Birch, for his tireless work on *Undivided*. I am thrilled to have the book published by Purposeful Design and thank Steve Babbitt and the ACSI administration for their interest in the topic.

I acknowledge, with appreciation, my daughter, Dr. Debbie MacCullough, for her continued feedback and development of the approach addressed in this book. Most of all, I appreciate that she, too, is teaching teachers to use a worldview approach in biblical integration. There are many more who should be acknowledged—family, professors, and colleagues, with whom I have lived, studied, and worked.

Most of all, I am thankful to the Lord for allowing me to serve Him in the field of education for many years. *"Teach me your way, Lord, that I may rely on your faithfulness; give me an undivided heart, that I may fear your name."* —Psalm 86:11

Introduction

This book is an expansion of my 1999 booklet, *Developing a Worldview Approach to Biblical Integration,* which put into writing two workshops on the topic. For several years, delegates had requested a written guide to use in their schools. The booklet was revised in 2008, 2010, and 2012 and translated into several languages: Spanish, Portuguese, Chinese, Thai, and parts in Russian. Some of the information in that first booklet will reappear in this book.

When I was first conducting workshops on Christian worldview thinking, there were numerous scholarly books written by Christian authors on the topic. Most of these compared the Christian theistic worldview to contemporary worldviews. The work of Francis Schaeffer, which I encountered in my graduate program at Wheaton College, became a primary resource for my early thinking on the subject.

The concept of worldview thinking took hold in the Christian community in the USA during the 1970s and early 1980s, a time of rapid growth for the Christian school movement. During the same time period, there were Christians writing on spiritual formation and the process of developing a Christian mind. However, there was little written on *how* to develop Christian worldviews in an academic setting.

At conferences and conventions, I shared what I had done in the classroom to promote biblical integration in the strategic design of the school *curriculum.* My classroom experiences carried over into teaching at the college level, where I continued to develop the model. Finally, in response to the nudging and encouragement of several key Christian educators and seminar delegates, I put my approach in writing. This book is offered as an expansion of that first work, adding a more comprehensive look at a worldview approach to *thinking* and to the process of developing true biblical integration in academic institutions.

This book will cover issues that were not examined in the original booklet. It will briefly address the current barriers to integrating biblical worldview in the curriculum of a Christian school or college and reasons why worldview integration is so important. The book expands the descriptions of *worldview* and *curricular integration*, encouraging teachers at any level to help students connect to, and distinguish from, a biblical Christian worldview. This educator-thinking process is essential to the approach described in this book. In addition, the second section of the book will briefly address worldview thinking as critical thinking and present an overall model for teaching any subject at any level (based upon human learning theory that answers the questions, "What is a human being?" and "How do we learn?"). Biblical integration is developed as integral to the regular curriculum; as such it must be considered part of the learning event and be subject to the basic answers to the questions about human nature and learning. A worldview approach to biblical integration must be addressed as a *natural part of the curriculum.*

The book is specifically written for educators, teachers, and administrators: those who influence the design of the curriculum in Christian educational institutions. However, the book may encourage worldview thinking for Christians who are serving in any setting. The primary goal of the book is to provide a working model for biblical worldview integration that is directed primarily toward the personal development of the educator, a necessity for effective curricular integration.

The book is divided into two sections: first, the background needed to understand worldview thinking as it relates to the teaching approach taken in this book; and second, a practical model that arises from this particular approach. The approach is designed to help educators and schools become more effective in the task of helping students and teachers think and act out of a Christian worldview as the integrating core for all life *and* learning. Settings that may benefit from the approach are Christian schools or other private international schools, home schools, colleges or universities, church schools, and even, in a limited way, public schools in which Christian teachers are employed.

One

What Is a Worldview?

The term *worldview* enters the conversation of sports figures, political aspirants, news commentators, and writers, and may be found in blogs, tweets, and other social media daily. Often, it is used to label a divergent viewpoint: "They are coming at this from a different worldview" is a common statement today.

This current, rather sloppy usage of the term can be confusing. In order to understand a worldview approach to biblical integration, one must first be clear as to what constitutes a worldview and how that relates to biblical integration as a *curricular* issue.

Several common definitions, more targeted than the popular usage of the term, will be provided. From these, a composite working definition will be developed upon which to build a framework for the development of a *worldview approach* to biblical integration.

A Personal Journey in Defining Worldview

Worldviews are concerned with the basic, foundational questions of life: Who am I? Why am I here? What is the purpose, if any, for the human being? Must we create a purpose? Disasters such as war or hate crimes precipitate a common worldview question: "What is wrong with our world?" A worldview answers these questions, among others.

Here is a typical dictionary definition of the term worldview, taken from the *American Heritage Dictionary of the English Language, 5th Edition*: "The overall perspective from which one sees and interprets the world. A collection of beliefs about life and the universe held by an individual or a group" (2011).

My early attempts to define and use the concept of a worldview in a school setting were before the term exploded in popularity. The first education-related definition that I encountered was in a resource book for sixth grade social studies. In *The Human Adventure* (1971), worldviews were "controlling ideas"—ideas or beliefs that control our actions. The book addressed nine questions answered by a worldview. Finding and using these questions was, for me, the beginning of the development of a worldview approach to biblical integration. My early definition of a worldview was simply "the controlling ideas or beliefs that answer the big questions of life and guide one's thinking and acting." I have modified that original definition by reading others on the topic since that time; however, that definition served as a beginning point.

After graduation from the Wheaton College graduate program, I fully intended to enter public education when my husband and I moved back to Philadelphia. However, at the invitation of my pastor, I ended up interviewing for a position in a Christian school. The school was seeking an interim principal because the current principal had been diagnosed with a life-threatening disease. I took the position. This came with obvious responsibilities—developing a PE program and a library were first on the to-do list—but I had a deeper concern: what I should do differently in a Christian school than in a public school.

After a new permanent administrator was hired and my own children were both in school (preschool and first grade), I began to teach full-time, but the question stuck with me. Which aspects of the *curriculum* would be a distinguishing marker for truly Christian education? The journey to understand biblical integration began. I started with a "questions" approach, leading the class in answering the nine "controlling idea" questions for Christianity. This is how I began a worldview approach to biblical integration in a school setting. I have continued to develop the model ever since and have personally found this approach very natural and enriching.

A Sampling of Christian Definitions of "Worldview"

In *Creation Regained*, Dutch theologian Albert Wolters defines a worldview as "the comprehensive framework of one's basic beliefs about things" (2005). "Things," in his view, includes *everything* in our life and world "about which we can have beliefs." In Wolters' discussion of worldviews, he differentiates between a general philosophy of life, a theology, and a worldview. Wolters writes:

> Whatever its semantic history, the term "worldview" (or its equivalent "world-and-life view") seems to pinpoint a useful distinction between philosophy as a methodologically

rigorous academic discipline ... and the commonsense perspective on life and the world, the "system of values" or "ideology," which in one form or another is held by all normal adult human beings regardless of intelligence or education. In this sense, worldview does indeed precede science, and is therefore quite different from philosophy in the strictly theoretical sense.... For Christian philosophers, the obvious implication is that they must seek to orient their philosophizing to a Christian worldview. Or to put the case a bit more strongly and accurately, the Christian must seek to philosophize *on the basis of the Christian worldview*—that is, the biblical worldview. (In Hart, Hoeven, and Wolterstroff 1983; emphasis added)

Using the above description of a worldview and a philosophy of life, it should be evident that most humans may not have a philosophy of life, but all have a worldview. Worldview precedes the development of a general philosophy—or an educational philosophy, for that matter. A philosophy has been analyzed, systematized, and intentionally accepted as a rigorous academic discipline. Worldviews are often messier and held without significant conscious critique. The development of worldview thinking is vital to all Christian school educators who desire to operate out of a distinctively Christian philosophical base, and it begins with one's current worldview beliefs, regardless of background in philosophy or theology. All teachers, then, can begin to develop a worldview approach to biblical integration—even those without formal seminary or philosophical education.

In *Christian Contours*, Douglas Huffman states that a worldview "consists of all the beliefs about reality that we accept to be true" (2011). Worldview beliefs are sometimes called "truth claims." Each person holds beliefs about the world and life thought to be true.

When I began to teach at the college level, *The Universe Next Door* by James Sire helped me frame what I was trying to do with worldview integration. He describes worldview as "a set of presuppositions (assumptions which may be true, partially true, or entirely false) which we hold (consciously or subconsciously, consistently or inconsistently) about the basic make-up of our world" (2004).

In earlier editions, Sire had written that a worldview is a set of understandings or concepts "that work to provide a coherent frame of reference for all of thought and action." In the fifth edition, he added that a worldview is:

... a commitment, a fundamental orientation of the heart, that can be expressed as a *story* or in a set of presuppositions ... about the basic constitution of reality, and that provides the foundation on which we live and move and have our being. (2009)

Sire added the concept of a worldview as a foundational *story*. This concept is powerful in that the structure of the Bible is, in part, a vast story beginning at creation, continuing through God's revelation to and relationship with fallen humanity, and concluding with His planned restoration. Within that story, there are smaller stories of real people, places, and events—but they are all connected to the larger story.

A worldview is often described as a narrative that helps humans think through their own story. In our postmodern world, there is little or no place for metanarratives that tell a universal story such as the one found in the Bible. Albert Mohler, a theological seminary president, challenges this thinking in "The Christian Worldview as Master Narrative."

> But, from beginning to end, biblical Christianity is a master narrative. Biblical Christianity is not only a faith that involves essential truths; it is the story of God's purpose to redeem humanity and to bring glory to Himself. This narrative is revealed to us as a comprehensive master story that is as vast as the cosmos and so detailed as to include every atom and molecule of creation. (2010)

In one sense, then, developing a biblically Christian worldview is the task of every Christian. We must evaluate our own worldview assumptions and beliefs by the standard of God's bigger story.

Worldview: A Composite Definition

> A worldview is one's foundational *beliefs*, thought to be *true*, which answer life's biggest questions about *reality, knowledge, and values* and form a coherent frame of reference for thinking and acting.

The answers to the big questions of life become the "controlling ideas" in one's thinking and acting. The set of beliefs should form a coherent framework that gives meaning to everything we do and helps us to understand who we are, why we are here, and where we are going. They inform the story of our lives. Answers to worldview questions form a perspective: a lens through which we view God, ourselves, the external world, everyday life, ongoing history, knowledge, moral and long-term decision making, death, and destiny.

The composite definition raises additional questions, however. How would a person know whether or not his or her beliefs are true? Could they be partially true, or even false? And what is the measure for truth? Is there a reality that exists outside the knowing and believing mind, or does the individual person create his or her own reality? Is there a metanarrative to use as a touchstone for forming a reliable framework? Are worldview beliefs more of a "heart" issue or a "mind" issue? These additional questions are usually embedded in a person's worldview, consciously or subconsciously. Some of these questions will be addressed briefly in this book as we look at a sampling of worldviews.

ACTIVITY

Research the use of the term "worldview" since the mid-1800s. Pay particular attention to the German word *Weltanschauung*.

Consider definitions used by various worldviews to see how they are similar and how they differ. How would a naturalist, an existentialist, a pantheist, or a postmodernist define worldview? What questions, if any, are addressed? Which of the questions are presented as foundational?

A Questions Approach to Biblical Integration

The approach taken in this book is a worldview *questions* approach, which is becoming more and more popular today because of the aspects of cognition that seem to flourish in response to questions that are crafted for more than simple recall. Satisfying answers can transform the human mind.

I am convinced that many Christian teachers, administrators, and parents know biblical answers to worldview issues without knowing the questions to ask; therefore, they have little structure in developing biblical integration. In order to develop a structure that promotes worldview integration in the strategic design of the curriculum, I have selected the eight questions provided in *The Universe Next Door*—questions I have used for more than 30 years.

1. What is prime reality—the ultimate or foundational reality?

2. What is the nature of external reality, that is, the world around us?

3. What is a human being?

4. What happens to a person at death?

5. Why is it possible to know anything at all?

6. How do we know what is right and wrong?

7. What is the meaning of human history?

8. What life commitments are consistent with these beliefs?

Compare Sire's questions to the ones found in *The Human Adventure*. These questions do not mention God until question seven, revealing something of the authors' secular worldview:

1. What is the world and the universe? (What is it made of? How is it made? What can our senses tell us about it?)

2. What should human beings try to do with their lives? (Why are we here? What is our aim? What are our rights and duties?)

3. How can men and women know what is good and what is bad, or what is right and what is wrong?

4. Are human beings mainly good, or mainly bad, or a mixture of good and bad?

5. What is happiness? How can men and women find happiness?

6. Is there life after death?

7. Does God (or do gods) exist?

8. Does God (or do gods) care about human beings?

9. Are any of the controlling ideas of this particular people shared with other people? Are some shared with all men and woman?

In *Saving Leonardo*, Nancy Pearcey expresses an approach to worldview integration using the framework of creation, fall, and redemption. This is a popular approach used to think about the Christian "story." Pearcey adds a series of *questions* to the creation/fall/redemption framework in order to guide the reader.

> Every religion offers an interpretation of the world, a worldview, a counterpart to the biblical narrative of creation, fall, redemption. Translated into worldview terms, creation refers to the theory of origins: *Where did we come from? What is ultimate reality?* Fall refers to the problem of evil: *What's wrong with the world, the source of evil and suffering?* Redemption asks, *How can the problem be fixed? What must I do to become a part of the solution?* These are the three foundational questions that every religion, worldview, or philosophy seeks to answer." (2010; emphasis added)

In the introduction to this book, I shared my early curiosity about how one might accomplish biblical integration in a school setting. That question, combined with my desire to see young people grow in their love for the Lord, led to the development of the approach in this book. The worldview framework espoused here is a *Christian worldview.*

There are other very worthwhile approaches to biblical integration. The one I share here is one that has proved effective in helping teachers who lack a formal biblical education but know what the Bible says about the major questions of life. In addition, they desire to share those answers with others, so that student and teacher may, together, love and serve the Lord with undivided hearts. The questions approach should help teachers become comfortable in trying to infuse a Christian worldview into the regular curriculum they teach by connecting what fits with a Christian view of things and distinguishing what does not.

Other biblical integration models can be used in conjunction with this approach. One such approach is the story of creation, fall, redemption, and restoration. Harold Klassen, a former student of mine, identifies a fourth stage of the story, "fulfillment," in his book, *Visual Valet*. Other approaches may use biblical principles related to subject areas, which complements the questions approach.

No Excuses!

When I started sharing the model presented in this book many years ago, Christian school teachers said, "I can't do biblical integration because I never formally studied the Bible in seminary or college." I was sure that a lack of formal study shouldn't impede them and set out to design an approach that would not demand formal education in theology or philosophy. A worldview approach does, however, demand that a Christian know the basic biblical answers to life's biggest questions. It requires constant growth, study, and evaluation of one's own worldview. Teacher and student must integrate their worldviews together, cooperatively measuring truth and reality by the standard of God's Word.

The approach shared here is meant to be *integral* to the regular curriculum, not tacked on; it thus becomes a part of the critical thinking activities designed by the teacher for the student in any given content area. In my own experience, students enjoy the processing activities that promote worldview thinking. "Tacked-on devotionalizing" leads to boredom or dismissive behaviors.

How Are Worldviews Developed?

In order to promote a worldview approach to integration, it is helpful to understand how worldviews are developed. We all have a worldview, no matter how old we are; we begin developing one from the first moment we interact with those around us.

This was brought home to me in 1980, when John Lennon was murdered on the streets of New York City. During an interview, Lennon's preschool-aged son, Sean, said, "Now Daddy is part of God. I guess when you die you become much more bigger, because you're part of everything" (Cott and Doudna 1982).

Sean had already begun to develop a pantheistic worldview. Why and from where? Those who know even a little about his parents will recall their pantheistic leanings. Sean had absorbed the Eastern views of his parents.

Humans develop a view of reality (worldview) from social and cultural forces that interact with the individual.

In the interactive process of development, the mind begins to form answers to important questions: "Who am I as a human being? Why am I here on Earth, in this family, in this country or town, with this color of skin? Is there a God? Why can't I see Him? What happens to my grandparents when they die? Who made the flowers and trees, the ocean and land, the birds, my dog, and me? How did they come to be?" Children may not ask these questions aloud, but they are absorbing the answers from everyone around them and later from books, media, and school textbooks.

Using curriculum activities to address worldview questions brings these accumulated beliefs to the fore, allowing teachers to identify disparities between the Christian worldview and other worldviews. Curriculum activities can trigger answers students have never examined—answers that may be true, partially true, or entirely false in the light of God's Word. This will open the way to developing a biblically informed, and hopefully transformed, worldview.

ACTIVITY

Think of questions (other than what happens when a person dies) that children might ask or ponder as they go through the first five or six years of their educational life. In Appendix One, I have included the questions posed in *The Universe Next Door*, adapted for young children. Early childhood teachers might benefit by reading the adaptations or writing their own.

Early in my experience, when I was teaching sixth and seventh grade in a Christian school, I asked a friend who taught theology at the local college to come to my class and answer questions, since the class was studying worldviews. At the end of the two hour session (which had been planned for just one hour), my theologian friend told me that in all of his years of teaching up to that day, he had never received as many interesting and difficult questions as the class posed to him.

Children do have questions about life, death, destiny, etc. The Christian school should be a place where students can explore the answers to these questions from God's perspective in a safe, loving, and caring community.

Multiple outside forces come into play in the development of a worldview:

- Parents
- Siblings
- Relatives
- Community
- Church
- School
- Media
- Government
- Geographical region
- Culture

It is important to know that when children enroll in a pre-kindergarten, they already have a developing worldview, that is, some answers to life's biggest questions. (Sean Lennon was just five years old when he articulated his developing pantheistic worldview.) This makes the task of biblical worldview integration significant, especially in the early years. It is not just a task for middle school, high school, or college teachers; by the time students reach high school, many more social and cultural forces have influenced their beliefs.

The first premise of this book is that all of our students have a worldview. In fact, in casual conversations you will recognize answers to the basic questions of life. For instance, on an online forum about life after death, a user wrote:

> I don't believe there is a beyond. I see ourselves as nothing more than fleshy robots with our minds as the software to run it ... It's hard for me to imagine, let alone believe in a place for us to go after we die because I don't think there is an us anymore at that point ... I am *hilariously* superstitious however! It's annoying, they're all obviously false ... a part of me blames my depressing middle school and high school experiences from when I broke a mirror, etc. (http://forums.penny-arcade.com/discussion/108548/do-you-have-any-metaphysical-beliefs)

Which of the eight questions are addressed in this one little paragraph?

- *What is a human being?* A fleshy robot—a machine.

- *Is there life after death?* No.

- *What is the nature of knowing?* There is confusion on this issue: "superstitious," "I can't imagine," "I can't believe."

- *What is ultimately real?* Only matter.

One can find worldview statements expressed in cartoons; in media posts on YouTube, TV, Facebook, and Twitter; and in curriculum materials and resources designed for your classroom. The questions approach gives the teacher a framework for integrating worldviews into the curriculum. Answering the major worldview questions and incorporating those answers into the metanarrative God reveals in His Word promotes a robust Christian worldview in students.

ACTIVITY

Retrieve definitions or descriptions of the term "worldview" as used by writers espousing various non-Christian worldviews (postmodernism, pantheism, atheism) and compare these to the composite definition used here.

Two

A Brief Historical View of Curricular Integration

Biblical worldview integration in an academic setting must be understood as a function of the *curriculum*. During the twentieth and twenty-first centuries, the integrated curriculum has swung on a pendulum, alternately condemned as a "corruption of sound educational practices" or lauded as an answer to the shortcomings in the educational enterprise.

Curricular Integration in Schooling

The first major push to resolve the growing fragmentation of the K–12 curriculum in schools came in the 1920s with John Dewey's Progressive movement. The early years of the movement stressed the societal benefit of education, as opposed to individual benefit that would later enter educational philosophy. Modern-day curricular wars have been fought over whether schooling exists for society or for personal development. Both philosophies have found curricular integration useful, though other educators, concerned about a diminished emphasis on content, reject the notion of curricular integration altogether.

Curricular integration has been part of educational conversation in Western school education for almost 100 years. It is still a prominent topic today in most teacher education curricula.

Recently, educators have revisited *Ends and Means* by Aldous Huxley, which addressed the weaknesses of education in the early twentieth century, focusing specifically on the two popular educational systems of the day: the academic school and the technical school. Neither style of education bore the fruit for which Huxley, a humanist, hoped:

Many of those who are able to stay the course of an academic education emerge from the ordeal either as parrots, gabbling remembered formulas which they do not really understand; or, if they do understand, as specialists, knowing everything about one subject and taking no interest in anything else; or, finally, as intellectuals, theoretically knowledgeable about everything, but hopelessly inept in the affairs of ordinary life. Something analogous happens to the pupils of technical schools. They come out into the world, highly expert in their particular job, but knowing very little about anything else and having *no integrating principle in terms of which they can arrange and give significance to such knowledge as they may subsequently acquire.* (1937; emphasis added)

Huxley goes on to suggest that a good education "is supposed to be simultaneously a device for fostering intelligence and the source of a principle of integration."

Huxley found Western education lacking because it was fragmented. Education of the day did not enhance the human as a whole person. He was concerned that the integrating core of education, if any, was mainly scientific naturalism, which left out the human as a unique being. If human beings are simply part of the material universe, he wrote, one "doesn't see why [humans] shouldn't be handled as other parts of the material universe are handled: dumped here, like coal or sand, made to flow there, like water, 'liquidated' ... like so much ice over a fire." He called for a curriculum with an integrating principle for the entire educational enterprise. Rejecting the dehumanizing philosophy of scientific naturalism, Huxley proposed humanity itself as the integrating core.

Huxley's book was reprinted in 2012, and is now experiencing a must-read status for those interested in curricular integration. Readers have remarked how up-to-date this 1937 work sounds. Today, however, the popular integrating principle is not the dehumanizing scientific naturalism that Huxley denounced, but rather multiple principles provided by alternative worldviews, most of which (intentionally or by default) propose the *individual self* as an integrating core.

Early Attempts to Develop Curricular Integration

Curricular integration has oscillated between being embraced and being ostracized in education, depending on the dominant educational philosophy of the day. The pioneers of curricular integration, intent on teaching students the value of education in a democracy, developed lessons to help students make sense of their ongoing schooling. Social studies served as the core for this society-focused education. Later, the language arts replaced social studies, only to be supplanted by science and math in the early 1960s, after the Soviet Union launched Sputnik.

Naturalism, and its focus on science, dominated educational reform for a time, and the curriculum fragmented again. Values education was relegated to the home, schools were for academics, and teaching was a scientific enterprise. Behaviorism reigned supreme as the scientific theory of learning. The curriculum was to be objective and scientific. There was to be little integration of cultural values. The humanities, existing outside the scientific field, were not a primary focus. America tested the values-neutral school curriculum and found it wanting.

Early progressivism's emphasis on society met a challenge in existentialism, and the pendulum soon swung back toward personal development and personal choice. The humanities, though still not the major focus, were welcomed back into the curriculum.

Recently, the standards-based curriculum has come under fire for fragmenting education, reducing knowledge to bits and pieces of disparate content and trivializing content with high-stakes tests. The current innovation, the Common Core, has also come under fire. Educators promoting the Common Core assert that it combines the strong content of the standard-based curriculum with a focus on critical thinking and curricular integration, but this focus may not satisfy the critics. The integrating core—the knowledge thought to be most worth knowing—is usually the critical issue. In truth, curricular design is a philosophical matter!

Selecting the Integrating Principle in Curricular Integration

It was Herbert Spencer who wrote in the mid-1800s, "Before there can be a rational curriculum, we must settle which things it most concerns us to know.... We must determine the relative value of knowledges" (in Knight, Spencer 1909). Each philosophical perspective will emphasize different subject matter as the "knowledge most worth knowing," the integrating core that provides meaning for the curriculum as a whole and fortifies the understood purpose for education. As a naturalist, Spencer chose science.

Some of the curricular cores that have been championed in the twenty-first century are math and science; classical literature; self-esteem, creativity, choosing and decision-making; foundational knowledge and basic skills; and technology. These cores reflect some of the major educational philosophies of the past 100 years still espoused today: essentialism, perennialism, behaviorism, progressivism, and educational humanism.

We live in a pluralistic society; there will always be controversy concerning the value of certain knowledge over other knowledge. Christian schools, however, should not be tethered to the back and forth swing promoted by the major cultural worldview. Christian schools must affirm what knowledge is most worth knowing and how that will impact the design of the curriculum. What will be the core around which all other knowledge is integrated, appreciated, evaluated, and used? What knowledge gives meaning to all of life and learning and how can this knowledge be effectively woven into the curriculum?

Some Christian school leaders understand the integrated curriculum controversy in terms of the war between content and personal/social development and been accordingly skeptical about curricular integration. Some have turned against curricular integration after experiencing it at a public school, where the integrating core conflicted with their Christian worldview. This has led to a gross misunderstanding of *biblical* integration; some schools practice biblical integration that is little more than chapel, Bible class, or attaching a devotional to a lesson—further dissociating biblical truth from the curriculum.

Cornelius Plantinga writes to young college students about bringing all parts of life—including education—under the lordship of Christ in *Engaging God's World.*

> No matter how a Christian college plans to integrate faith, learning, and service, it will never just conduct education-as-usual—not if it is serious about Christian higher education. It won't even do education-as-usual with Bible classes tacked on, or education-as-usual with prayers before class, or education-as-usual with a service-learning component and a 10 o'clock chapel break. No, a solidly built Christian college will rise from its faith in Jesus Christ and then explore the height and depth, the length and breadth of what it means to build on this faith ... for a lifetime of learning.

What is true at the college level is certainly true at the elementary, middle, and high school levels.

In the 1970s, Christian schools stood completely opposed to the fragmented curriculum of public education. The battle for the minds of children from Christian homes was a battle for the concept of wholeness and integrity at a time when public schools, by design, endorsed neutrality in values. The experiment of a value-neutral curriculum had separated various domains of knowledge from one another and from values of any sort. There was no publically accepted integrating principle. Public education strove not to offend the worldviews of American families—though this supposed "neutrality," perhaps unintentionally, promoted some worldviews above others.

Christian educators and parents saw the need for an integrating core. We did not want our children to be split in their thinking—capable of switching from secular to sacred on demand; we wanted them to be whole. We saw no false dichotomy between secular and sacred. To that generation, all of life and learning were related to one's worldview, and for the Christian school, that worldview was biblical. Though we championed the view, we did not know how to promote biblical worldview integration in the curriculum.

Scholarly Contributions

Today, many public school educators are standing firm against the fragmentation caused by the teach-to-the-test standards movement. It seems to some that education has regressed to the incomplete learning science of the behaviorist—a theory which further segments knowledge without building connections among the disciplines. Thus, one of the popular themes of public education is the need for an integrating core around which all of life and learning can be organized. Knowledge must be viewed as unified, whole, and connected. Fragmentation has not worked. Researchers in curriculum design have noted that we have produced specialists who cannot solve problems or make decisions outside their narrow field. In the recent past, we have produced scientists who have never taken a philosophy course and do not recognize their own assumptions. We have graduated lawyers and business administrators who have never taken a course in ethics or had ethics integrated into their curriculum.

Counselors and therapists today realize that many humans are *disintegrated*. Flagrant relativism has left the human ship without a rudder. Many believe in everything; therefore, they believe in nothing, as Alan Bloom noted in *The Closing of the American Mind* (1987). Believing in nothing, he inferred, led to a closed mind rather than an open mind. Many of us have been led to believe that a person who knows what she believes is close-minded. According to Bloom, the opposite is true.

The lack of strongly held beliefs has diminished the process of critical thinking because there is no standard by which to make a rational judgment. Lack of basic beliefs has led to incoherence and the shriveling of ethical boundaries. This problem, noted by astute writers in the 1980s, became more visible by the end of the twentieth century and early twenty-first century, as we began to read daily of cyberbullying, knock-out (K.O.) gangs, school shootings, and gang wars. Human life is being devalued. The call for an integrated curriculum—one that values life, unifies learning, and inspires respect for others—is not limited to religious schools only.

Moving into the Twenty-First Century

In his final State of the Union address at the end of the twentieth century, President Clinton declared that we must teach values to our school children—but the question is, and has always been, what values should we teach? There is a crisis. We know we need values-based schooling; however, in an attempt to offend no one, we have removed core values—especially Christian values—from school curriculum. Are we reaping the results? While moral education is not the sole aspect of biblical worldview integration, it is part of it. Worldview questions can be organized under the general philosophical categories of metaphysics (reality), epistemology (knowing), and axiology (valuing): moral education fits under the general category of axiology. Moral education ought to be part of worldview education, but it is not the be-all and end-all some Christian schools have taken it to be. Character education is necessary, but not sufficient, in total worldview development.

One of the pivotal books in the 1990s that addressed the problems of American schools was *Politics, Markets, and America's Schools*, by John Chubb and Terry Moe. Their goal was to identify the schools that excelled at educating students and isolate which of those schools' practices could be adopted by schools nationwide. Their findings indicated that private schools educated students better than public schools did. This revelation encouraged public schools to adopt some qualities of private schools, such as polity and management practices, which are still used by charter schools today. Their findings also fueled the fires of the choice movement and opened the door to include private schools in the tax support equation, though this idea has yet to come to fruition in the United States.

Chubb and Moe concluded that private schools do not have to be all things to all people; they succeed by finding a niche and appealing to a specialized segment of the market. To Chubb and Moe, the obvious way to do this is through the strategic design of the *curriculum*. They drew a major conclusion about private education when they wrote:

> In the private sector, schools do not have to be all things to all people. To be successful, they need to find their niche—a specialized segment of the market to which they can appeal and attract support. The obvious way to do this is through the *strategic design of their curriculum*…. Their goals are also more likely to have true *intellectual coherence*— for they are not ad hoc collections of value-impositions, but packages that are consciously designed to constitute an *integrated* whole. The market allows and encourages its schools to have distinctive, well-defined "missions." (1990; emphasis added)

Intellectual coherence, it seems, is accomplished through the strategic design of the *curriculum*. It is planned—not just theoretical or spontaneous! A worldview provides a touchstone by which to evaluate new knowledge. It leads to a more open-minded person who can grow academically and examine knowledge in any area. Close-mindedness, however, is a consequence of rampant relativism as Bloom warned. But integration is a *curricular issue*, not just a mission statement!

Chubb and Moe did not set out to promote private schools but to find elements that would help the youth of America connect schooling to life in general. Their research did spur the development of a hybrid sort of schooling: the charter school, a public school with a specific and targeted mission around which to organize learning. Private schools can do even better in this regard.

A Potent Force in Education

Just five years after the writing of *Politics, Markets, and America's Schools,* the Association of Supervision and Curriculum Development—the most prestigious curriculum organization in the world—commissioned a group of educators to address coherency and integration in the public school curriculum. The educators compiled their findings in the ASCD's 1995 yearbook, *Toward a Coherent Curriculum.* The book delivered a fascinating indictment of the fragmented curriculum and lack of intellectual coherency our youth face in the classroom, claiming that the current curriculum contributed to lack of connection between learning and life. The group of educators called for new approaches to integration. The editor, James Beane, writes:

> A "coherent" curriculum is one that holds together, that makes sense as a whole; and its parts, whatever they are, are unified and connected by the sense of the whole.... This kind of coherence will open up possibilities for the integration of educational experiences.... That is, when the curriculum offers a sense of purpose, unity, relevance and pertinence—when it is coherent—young people are more likely to *integrate educational experiences into their scheme of meaning,* which in turn broadens and deepens their understanding of themselves and the world. (1995; emphasis added)

Notice that an integrated curriculum does not lead to a narrow education but rather to one that "broadens and deepens" one's understanding of the self and the world. In order for there to be integration of schooling with life, there must be something that promotes coherency—an integrating core that holds the curriculum together.

> The search for coherence involves long-standing issues in the politics of *curriculum* because it must involve decisions about what ideas or themes will hold the curriculum together. The question of what the "glue" is raises other questions, such as "Whose glue is it?" and "Who decides what the glue is?" (1995; emphasis added)

The contributing authors all agreed that curricular coherency was the essential element that made school learning worthwhile. Beane admitted that, because the "big ideas" that hold the planned curriculum together are expressions of value, "it is worth asking whether it is possible to reach any kind of reasonable consensus regarding possibilities for coherence."

Beane inferred that it is probably not possible to have a specific integrating core in public schools, making true intellectual coherency elusive. Allan Bloom might add that this is one of the reasons high school students enter universities without the knowledge base and conviction necessary for critical thinking.

What a sad conclusion for schools—but not for the Christian school! Christian schools should know exactly what holds the curriculum together: biblical answers to life's biggest questions.

Herbert Spencer declared that understanding and adopting the knowledge most worth knowing preceded the development of a rational curriculum. For the Christian educator, a unified, effective curriculum is driven by biblical truth; it values human beings as image-bearers of God and encourages them to flourish.

A Renewed Interest

In *The Question of God*, Harvard psychology professor Armand M. Nicholi compares the lives of Sigmund Freud and C. S. Lewis. These two great thinkers were alike in many ways: both had difficult childhoods and exposure to religion, and both became atheists in their late teen years, though Lewis abandoned his atheism in his early thirties. Nicholi's book highlights the differences between Freud's and Lewis's worldviews—atheistic naturalism and theism, respectively—on the topics of love, sex, suffering, death, and happiness, among others. Nicholi claims that Lewis's "spiritual" worldview had a positive personality effect while Freud's atheistic naturalism had a negative personality effect. These effects were especially pronounced in how the two faced life difficulties and death. Nicholi writes:

> Our worldview informs our personal, social, and political lives. It influences how we perceive ourselves, how we relate to others, how we adjust to adversity, and what we understand to be our purpose. Our worldview helps to determine our values, our

ethics, and our capacity for happiness. It helps us understand where we come from, our heritage; who we are, our identity; why we exist on this planet, our purpose; what drives us, our motivation; and where we are going, our destiny. (2002)

Nicholi conducted research using Harvard undergraduates who, like C.S. Lewis, had a "religious conversion" while at Harvard. His findings were significant in demonstrating the positive personality effects in those students: the religious conversion not only steered students away from drugs, alcohol, and sexual promiscuity, but also lessened their "existential despair" and "preoccupation with the passage of time and apprehension over death." The conversion experience also correlated with improvements in academic performance, communication with parents, and relationships. While these results are correlative findings, it is interesting to note that a worldview shift may correlate with real-life positive relationships, functioning, and attitudes—worthy goals for Christian education. Nicholi's conclusions were a tacit affirmation of the worldview of the "believer."

Nicholi strongly encourages his students at Harvard to think clearly about the life implications of one's worldview because all worldviews cannot be true. In the case of Freud's atheistic naturalism and Lewis's theism, for instance, if one is true, the other *must* be false. Contemporary students' resistance to this concept makes pluralism one of the major barriers to biblical worldview integration.

While national laws in the USA forbid specific (sectarian) religious core values in public education, many social, political, and psychological scientists, aware of the need, are moving toward public attempts at curricular coherency. Christian schools should take up the banner for curricular integration with confidence and skill not only because of human cognitive and affective benefits, but because abundant life in Christ includes our academic life. Helping Christian schools do this is the purpose of this book.

ACTIVITY

1. What is the current state of curricular integration in the area in which you teach?

2. What is the current concept of curricular integration espoused at your school or in your teacher education program?

3. Is curricular integration currently being embraced or scorned? What evidence can you provide for this conclusion?

Three

Defining and Describing Curricular Integration

"Marti," my friend said, "I am furious! The school is talking about developing an integrated curriculum and I have been listening to the Christian radio commentators who say that this is a movement that will destroy good education and it is anti-Christian. What do you think of the integrated curriculum?"

I could only wonder where she had gotten her information—either the school in question had failed to describe the integrated curriculum, or my friend had picked up her opinions from biased sources. We chatted for a while, and the conversation was eye-opening. I had assumed curricular integration was well understood. I was wrong.

At times, we in Christian circles dismiss ideas and potential curricular changes without fairly evaluating them, just because they have been adopted and promoted in public education. This can be counterproductive to Christian education and one of the reasons that Christian teachers and administrators should be developing a philosophy of instruction informed by a Christian worldview. Educators need a cogent, thoroughly examined philosophy of education with which to evaluate new ideas. This chapter will offer a brief look at definitions and descriptions of curricular integration to help us frame what will be developed in the latter half of the book.

The General Concept of Integration

Take a minute to think of a definition for *integration* as it is used in media and in casual conversation. Write four or five descriptive words that come to mind when you think of the term and then write a definition that reflects how you currently use the terms *integration*, *integral*, or *integrate*. Compare your descriptive words to the dictionary definition below:

To incorporate into a larger unit; bringing together into a larger whole.

The Collins English Dictionary, among others, defines integration as "the act of combining or adding parts to make a unified whole." Dictionary.com offers some helpful bullet points:

1. To bring together or incorporate (parts) into a whole.

2. To make up, combine, or complete to produce a whole or a larger unit.

Notice the concept of bringing together *into a larger whole* in the definitions above. This idea will be helpful as we examine what we need to *do* as we design the Christian school curriculum for worldview integration. What is the "larger whole" in biblical worldview integration? Is it just the eight or so biblical answers to worldview questions, or does it include more? A Christian worldview includes not only the view of reality as God sees it but also the knowledge from any domain of study that fits with that view. All disciplines in the school curriculum are God-ordained as part of His creative order, whether science, mathematics, social sciences, physical and social activity, or the humanities. All have some residual characteristics of their original creative design in spite of human sin.

Worldview integration is a *connecting* process as well as a *distinguishing* process. Thus, a biblical worldview grows as the basic questions of life are answered by a biblical view and enhanced by knowledge found in any area. Views that fit with a biblical worldview fortify worldview development. This is the growing "larger whole." Further, when incompatible views are distinguished from a Christian view, the Christian view becomes more robust and distinctive in the mind. When knowledge found in specific areas clearly conflicts with Scripture, the distinguishing process acts as a contrast. When knowledge in specific areas clearly connects with a Christian biblical worldview, it serves as a complement, helping to expand the worldview. Students and the teacher develop a better understanding of people who hold to differing belief systems and can therefore appreciate them as human beings while distinguishing their own beliefs.

Integration in the Medical Profession

Merriam-Webster defines integration as "the coordination of mental processes into a normal effective personality or with the individual's environment." In this definition, integration leads to an effective, healthy personality.

The medical profession uses the term integration in relation to human health, paralleling Nicholi's research in *The Question of God*.

> When we observe Freud's life and the life of Lewis before and after his conversion, we can't help but observe how one's worldview has a profound impact on one's capacity to experience happiness. Lewis stated clearly that his pessimism and gloom were closely related to his atheism. His conversion experience changed his pessimism, gloom, and despair to joy, freedom from the burden of driving ambition, and many satisfying relationships. (2002)

Nicholi was curious to find out whether religious conversions "reflected pathology and a futile attempt to resolve severe inner conflict or escape reality" or something more. He writes that the students expressed a sense of joy and that a "newfound intense introspection made them more acutely aware—not less—of how far short they fell from the ideal of perfection their faith demanded."

One might think that this new knowledge would make them less happy and despair all the more, but it had the opposite effect: "[Converted students] spoke of spiritual resources that give strength and renewed hope and that foster a more open, more tolerant, and more loving spirit toward others. They referred frequently to the theological concepts of redemption and forgiveness as being instrumental in reducing their self-hatred." Other researchers have also found that those who suffer from depression but possess a spiritual worldview responded more quickly to treatment than those espousing a secular worldview.

In a recent edition of *Time* magazine, Mandy Oaklander summarizes the research of two scientists on the topic of why some people bounce back from difficult experiences better than others (June 2015). The concept is sometimes labeled "resilience." The article offered ten tips for developing resilience, the first of which was, "Develop a core set of beliefs that nothing can shake." I found this to be an amazing conclusion. The Christian worldview is a set of beliefs we can hold confidently because they have been revealed by God.

How might worldview integration impact the human personality and why might this be important in a Christian learning environment? The term itself may be of some help.

Integration and Integrity: How Are They Related?

The terms "integration" and "integrity" both come from the Latin root *integritas*. A key result of worldview integration is an integrated human personality, one that is healthy and whole. Integrity is the state of being one person in all circumstances—public or private, stressed or relaxed, happy or sad. Integrity is polemically opposed to the practical dualism of students who can be sacred in Bible class and secular on the basketball court. It is, in fact, a corrective to the secular/sacred divide itself.

It is no wonder, given the documented relationship between curricular integration and human flourishing, that in the last two decades we have heard the voices of educators calling for a return to the integrated curriculum. Scripture speaks to this issue as well. "The integrity of the upright guides them, but the unfaithful are destroyed by their duplicity" (Proverbs 11:3).

A key result of worldview integration is an integrated human personality. When Christian worldview integration occurs, the human being can experience wholeness and health, both intellectually and emotionally. Integration combats duplicity (divided thinking—speaking out of both sides of one's mouth) and hypocrisy (pretending to be something one is not).

Integration refers to human wholeness, as distinct from the disintegrated, dualistic beliefs that are the product of a sacred/secular divide. If indeed one of the goals of education is to help children and youth develop and flourish as persons of *integrity*, then curricular integration is vital, especially to those who teach in Christian institutions.

While most Christian institutions of learning have acknowledged the importance of worldview integration, not all are designing curriculum and practicing curricular integration in such a way that students develop wholeness and intellectual coherency. Schools should be purposive to that end. It is a worthy goal for all of society—not just the Christian school.

ACTIVITY

Research the popular definitions of *integration* as used in education and especially as used to describe an integrated curriculum.

Examples of "Integration"

The examples below have been written as illustrations of integration, both good and bad. Evaluate the first three examples according to the general concept of integration—"bringing together into a larger whole"—rather than more specific biblical integration.

Example One

A physics teacher has students memorize mathematical formulae, paying very little attention to physical science concepts. She claims to be integrating math with science.

Example Two

During autumn, a second grade teacher has her children color leaves for science class. She never mentions any science concepts related to color changes in leaves. She says she is integrating art with science.

Example Three

A fifth grade teacher uses a textbook program for science and never uses hands-on materials. He claims to be integrating reading with science.

If you evaluated these three attempts to integrate as substituting one subject for another, you would be correct.

In the first example, the teacher is right to use math in physics class—it is a necessity—but to avoid a focus on the physical science concepts is to turn physics into rote memorization of mathematical formulae. It does not bring together the two subjects into a larger whole.

The second teacher is on target in allowing her second graders to color leaves of various colors in science class; however, to avoid any science teaching related to why leaves change colors in the fall (even at a second grade level) substitutes coloring for science.

The third illustration depicts a necessary part of science teaching: teaching students to read and understand domain-specific vocabulary and concepts. However, science is a hands-on, concrete subject. It is the investigation into the natural world using the senses. Science teaching is not adequate unless it frequently includes hands-on activities (labs) and computer models. The teacher above is substituting reading for science.

The next illustrations are very similar to what might be used in a Christian school environment; they may even be found in curriculum guides. Do they fit the definition of *integration*? Are they biblical integration?

Example Four

"When atoms lose their outer electrons, they take on a positive charge. The more they lose, the greater the positive charge. When a person accepts Christ as Savior, he or she loses sin and takes on a plus charge for God. The more we are dedicated, the more sin we lose, and the more we can positively serve God."

Example Five

"Light is produced in a variety of ways: a candle, a fire, a light bulb, a fluorescent bulb, a laser beam, a match, or a gas stove. A light bulb is often harsh if it has no shade, a fire is often too hot and dangerous, and a fluorescent bulb can often be 'shady' and too soft. A laser beam is direct, coherent, sharp, and hits the target. The light of a match doesn't last long. What is your Christian light like? Does it go out quickly? Is it shady in the sense that it is not clear as to purpose? Does it just flicker or is it too harsh? Does it go out quickly? Or is your light like the laser beam, consistent and coherent? Let's be laser beams in our Christian lives."

Neither of the above are examples of a worldview approach to biblical integration. Although there is nothing inherently wrong with using science ideas as analogs to scriptural truth *when the analogy is a good one*, this is not the case here.

What would the view in Example Four do to the concept of negative charges built into the design of nature by the Creator of the universe? Are not both positive and negative charges important in the universe? Would the activities above lead to intellectual coherency or to a division between science and something quasi-spiritual?

This sort of biblical integration substitutes a devotional for science rather than bringing together the science with a key concept from one's biblical worldview. How might this affect the mind of the student? Might it lead to a distorted view of the various sources and benefits of light and heat? I, for one, am glad that I do not have to use a laser to light a candle in my home. Singing "this little laser beam of mine, I am going to let it *zap, zap, zap*" might be fun for the kids, but does it lead to intellectual coherency?

These types of activity draw the mind away from science. The students are led to think more about the Christian life rather than uniting the science with a biblical perspective.

When we use a worldview approach with the above lessons on positive and negative charges and light sources, we might focus on the human, created in the image of God, with the capacity to discover and use God's creative order. The lesson might answer, in part, the worldview questions, "What is the nature of the external world?" and "What is the nature of the human being as we investigate and use the external world?"

The Integrated Curriculum

The curriculum is more than the textbook or materials. It includes the unit and lesson plans, the delivery, assessment procedures and follow-up, and the environment: in short, it includes everything planned by the teacher to promote learning. The integrated curriculum uses core knowledge to make connections between varied subjects and skills, making learning less fragmented. School and life in general will have more coherence. Biblical integration does not dismiss specific content by "substituting" an object lesson or analogy to teach a biblical truth. This practice divides knowledge into secular and sacred rather than bringing information together into a larger whole.

Describing an integrated curriculum has been a task for curricular theorists for more than 100 years. Over this period, theorists have offered several labels and definitions. The Association of Supervision and Curriculum Development (ASCD) has provided numerous articles on the integrated curriculum, often under various other labels (interdisciplinary learning, multidisciplinary learning, and thematic units, among others). These articles vary in their description of the integrated curriculum: some describe teachers from two or more subject areas teaming together for the teaching of a unit; others depict a classroom teacher tearing down the boundaries between subject areas in teaching a unit or topic, or subject matter teachers bringing together knowledge from another discipline to enhance their own discipline.

What kind of connections and distinctions are needed in the integrated curriculum? Connections across disciplines, connections to real life, and connections to one's worldview are all part of the planned integrated curriculum.

At the university where I teach, we explore together three types of integration:

1. *Subject-to-subject integration*: often called multi-disciplinary or interdisciplinary learning, and thematic units

2. *Subject-to-life integration*: stresses authentic learning and assessment that helps students to understand the connections between learning and everyday life

3. *Subject-to-worldview integration*: the teacher, "in the strategic design of the curriculum," plans the integration of a biblical worldview with the subjects of the school curriculum

Subject-to-subject and subject-to-life integration may occur in a public school classroom in the planning and delivery of the curriculum. In the U.S. and many other countries, however, robust worldview integration is largely limited to private schools.

The Integrated Curriculum Is Planned

An integrated curriculum begins with the learning plans. It is planned, not just spontaneous. The planned *environment* is also important. For effective learning to take place, students need to experience what I like to call "relaxed structure." They should be encouraged to express their ideas and listen respectfully. They should be free to get answers right, partially right, or wrong as part of the learning process. An effective learning community that promotes intellectual coherency *is* part of the curriculum—because the curriculum is everything planned to promote learning.

Westernized societies have successfully rid the government school curriculum of the Judeo-Christian integrating core espoused in early American education. It has been replaced with the fragmented "value-neutral" experiment that started in the 1960s and 1970s. However, educators who see the problem firsthand are attempting to promote coherency, meaning, and integration in order to motivate young people to see learning as part of life. Christian schools should be proactive in this endeavor—that means planning, preparing, and executing it!

A Practical Definition

In the early years of the Christian school movement, teachers needed a description of the integrated curriculum to know what to do in the development of biblically integrated lessons. I developed the following definition more than 30 years ago to help teachers see what the process of integration is all about. Curricular worldview integration is:

> Planning *curricular* activities that help the student think through subject matter and skill development in such a way as to develop the habit of connecting and contrasting all knowledge to their biblical worldview, the integrating core out of which an integrated Christian will think and act.

The working definition above presupposes that:

1. Educators understand the concept of a worldview.

2. Educators understand that worldview integration occurs in the students' thinking as they are challenged to compare and contrast beliefs.

3. The process leads to change in thought and actions; it is a learning event. Ideally, this way of thinking becomes a habit.

4. There is a method to teaching that is essential in promoting the process in students.

The goal of curricular biblical integration is for the student and teacher to develop a personal perspective or worldview that is informed by a biblical view of things. Curricular integration aims to promote the development of critical thinking. Strengthening their worldview will make students more open-minded and more intellectually coherent. Students will have a touchstone by which to judge information as true or false, bad or good. They will develop the habit of thinking biblically. They will also be encouraged to do additional study and research to expand their knowledge in both the Bible and in the subject area. Above all, the goal of curricular biblical integration is to promote loving the Lord with an undivided heart and living wholeheartedly for Him.

ACTIVITY

1. Using the terms "curriculum" and "integration," write one or two summary sentences that describe what a worldview approach to biblical integration looks like in a school.

2. How do you think subject-to-subject integration might contribute to a worldview approach to biblical integration? Why?

3. Select one of the examples of integration used in this chapter and defend why it is not an example of a worldview approach to biblical integration.

Four

The Need for Worldview Integration in Christian Education

The need for worldview-integrated education has been well documented in recent years as well as in the past. Over 100 years ago, Abraham Kuyper founded the Free University of Amsterdam, dedicated to the concept that "all of the sciences belong to Jesus Christ and must be studied in light of His Word" (Greene, 1977). As prime minister, Kuyper worked to develop a system of education in which public schools and Christian schools were funded equally with public monies. He fought for financial equality for educational choice for more than 40 years. The equal financial base for private and public schools was constitutionally established in the Pacification Act of 1917, just three years before Kuyper died. Christian schools were to be distinctively Christian in nature, dedicated to the integration of all the sciences with God's Word. This was Kuyper's gift to Christian parents in Holland.

Educator Albert Greene, who visited the Netherlands just sixty years after the establishment of the two-pronged system, observed that the equally funded public and private systems had become almost identical. Greene reported that the Minister of Education "was calling for a merger of the Christian and the secular schools because they are so much alike." What had happened to the once-vibrant Christian distinctive? While the Dutch had guaranteed freedom for the expression of diverse religious views in school choices and the Pacification Act guaranteed money so that parents had a true choice, the government could not guarantee Kuyper's goal of an educational system in which a biblical worldview was foundational to all learning. According to one of my former students, who had attended a Dutch Christian school in the late 1990s, neither Dutch school system is very "Christian" in philosophy.

Kuyper was interested in all levels of education. In his inaugural address at the university he founded, he spoke of the nature of the new school that he was undertaking. It was to be a school very different than the universities of the day. The world of higher education and the scientific naturalism prevalent at the time had apparently led school education to become "neutral" toward religion, promoting a dualism of secular and sacred. Kuyper wanted to counter the culture by establishing a choice for Christians in their academic pursuits as well as in their public, political, and social lives—a worthy goal, but not an easy one. This kind of education needed to be continually fueled by Christians who truly understood the integrated life.

The experiment in the Netherlands prompts some important questions for Christian educators in North America and around the globe. How can Christian schools worldwide provide and maintain a distinctively Christian education? What will prevent our Christian schools from becoming clones of secular or public education, with or without government money? What is the key distinctive of a truly Christian education? I submit to you that it is the effective practice of biblical worldview integration, an approach that leads to a Christian worldview.

The Impact of the Predominant Worldview

The need for biblical worldview thinking abounds in the general culture today. A renewed interest in the "spiritual realm" and the development of the whole person has been spawned by the growth of New Ageism and pantheistic worldview thinking. The rise of school violence in the last 25 years and the feelings of vulnerability in the wake of 9/11 have awakened an interest in the human spirit. Some in our culture ask, "Have we killed the innate goodness of humankind? Have we abandoned the spiritual part of the human being?"

Most of the popular concepts of "spirituality" are foreign to Christian thinking. Even so, Christian educational institutions can take advantage of the tenor of the day to restore wholeness and a more unified view of knowledge and life without succumbing to the negative influences of pervasive worldviews.

The sacred/secular divide has divorced beliefs and values from work, politics, and academic life, and personalism and self-centeredness have filled the vacuum. In reaction to the narrow epistemology of scientific naturalism, the "self" has become the core of the nation's worldview. Academia and the general public seem ripe for postmodernism and pantheism, both of which offer a spirituality meant to restore meaning to humankind. The focus on the self, the call to create one's own personal truth, promotes rampant relativism. It challenges not only atheistic naturalism but also the right of God to declare universal truth. The proposed secular cores are insufficient: there is a clear and inescapable need for solid Christian education.

The Twenty-First Century Anti-God Movement

Another reason that Christian educators should be interested in worldview integration today is the strong anti-God movement that has exploded in popularity. In 2007, the late Christopher Hitchens wrote the baldly-titled *God is Not Great* (originally subtitled *How Religion Poisons Everything*, but later changed to *A Case Against Religion*). Hitchens, seeing the decline of scientific materialism in the face of spirituality, argued for the permanent divorce of faith from public life—a divorce that results in the damaging sacred/secular divide.

Academia heard calls from Hitchens and others to expel from public life anything that relates to "religion," whether values, religious history, religious literature, or concepts of design in the natural world. However, Hitchens' real thrust was not really a dualism in life between secular and sacred, but a new culture of overt atheistic naturalism: a "renewed Enlightenment."

During the first decade of the twenty-first century, several atheist writers joined Hitchens in vocally condemning religious and spiritual worldviews. Daniel C. Dennett wrote *Breaking the Spell*, in which he argued that the prevalence of religion could be explained as a natural part of the survival process in evolution. In the same year, Richard Dawkins added *The God Delusion* to the growing body of atheist work.

But there is a strange conflict in the atheistic perspective: atheistic naturalists view religion as a harmful phenomenon, but also argue that it is a survival response. Naturalists who try to explain why humans are "still" religious explain religion in the context of naturalistic determinism, painting the religious as victims of their genetics and environment. On this victimhood basis, believers cannot be *responsible* for these atrocities, because they could not have done otherwise. But the atheist can't have it both ways—moral responsibility in one case and no responsibility in the other.

In his *Newsweek* article "The New Naysayers," Jerry Adler made an astounding observation about some of the current-day atheistic authors.

> These authors have no geopolitical strategy to advance; they're interested in the metaphysics of belief, not the politics of the First Amendment. It's the *idea of putting trust in God* they object to, not the motto on the nickel. This sets them apart from

America's best-known atheist activist, the late Madalyn Murray O'Hair, a controversial eccentric who won a landmark lawsuit against mandatory classroom prayers in 1963 and went on to found the group now called American Atheists. (2006; emphasis added)

Cultural Barriers

There are at least three worldviews currently impacting education: bold atheistic naturalism, Western formulations of pantheism, and a self-described "naturalistic pantheism." All three of these views vie for the minds and hearts of our youth. Westernized pantheism encourages turning inward to the self as the source of truth, legitimizing all beliefs, whether rational or not. This latter view seems to dominate media—especially entertainment media. The only exception is when someone disagrees with their view. Naturalistic pantheism tries to cushion the despair of deterministic naturalism with the language of pantheism, which "loves" and "worships" Mother Earth.

Our students are impacted by the culture, whether atheistic, naturalistic, pantheistic, or postmodernist, and so are we. We are "in the world" and must be vigilant to prevent intellectual incoherency caused by cultural trends. This is why we must be intentional in the development of a biblical worldview and continue to evaluate our core beliefs as new thought-forms enter the culture. There is very little homogeneity in beliefs, especially in the Western world. This can be a barrier to Christian living unless Christians practice biblical worldview thinking in public and private living, in social life, physical life, political life, *and* academic life.

Christian Schools Then and Now

Biblical integration was the hallmark of Christian education during the Christian school surge in the 1970s. Schools were passionate about helping families educate their children from a Christian perspective. Integration was welcomed, even championed, but the enthusiasm waned.

Curricular integration gained popularity in public schools and was somewhat demonized in Christian schools, squelching some of the early attempts at biblical integration. It appears that when an educational fad is adopted by a current cultural or education philosophy that contradicts biblical Christianity, we either tacitly abandon the concept itself or demonize it. What quality concepts have we abandoned to the secular world because they have been usurped by a philosophy that does not fit with biblical Christianity?

Coherency and Worldview Integration in a Christian School

The desire to develop biblical integration using a Christian worldview has led to school boards and administrators seeking to counter incoherency and champion the staying power of a biblical view for their students. "Integration of faith and learning," a typical phrase of the 70s and 80s, provided a common call for intentionality in the curriculum. This led some to believe that schools ought to use only Christian published materials. Others required their teachers to place some type of biblical statement—often a verse or prayer—on each lesson plan. But this is not true biblical worldview integration.

Today, administrators see the need to revisit biblical integration; they recognize that past efforts have not promoted a truly Christian worldview. Many schools ask me to present the approach in this book because "We simply are not doing biblical integration," or "Our teachers do not know what to do other than to tack on verses or pray before class or just leave this to the chapel period each week."

True intellectual coherency is only possible when life, learning, and private and public life are integrated with a cohesive worldview. Intellectual coherency is a function of worldview integration. Coherency alone is not the goal, however; we seek coherency that occurs around biblical truth claims and a worldview that is continually being informed and reformed by the Word of God.

The integrating core for the Christian is no mystery. However, some teachers have never understood practical worldview integration and are confused about how to accomplish it.

Bible-Centered, Christ-Centered, or What?

Christian education is described as Bible-centered or as Christo-centric. However, these labels do very little to help teachers incorporate biblical integration in the strategic design of the curriculum. Teachers often ask me, "Where do I begin in the Bible when the integrating core is the Bible?" Or, "If the curriculum is Christo-centric, do I just use the Gospels and the life of Christ?" I was challenged to find a more tangible approach to use with teachers. The pedagogical model developed in Chapter 11 answers the "how" of the Integrating Core Model, in which the integrating core is *biblical* answers to worldview questions.

Curricular Integration in Public Schools: Self or Society

In the public arena, the integrating principle of the curriculum has become the self, society, or some democratic version of reciprocity between the two. With all due respect for

American democracy and the role of the good human as a good citizen, the battles between those competing views have not produced coherency and integrated human personalities. What is a good person? Pluralistic thinking allows for several descriptions that are mutually exclusive. What is a good society? Again, different worldviews answer in mutually exclusive ways. These questions are best answered when the central theme is neither self nor society, but rather the God who made humankind to function as unique individuals in community. When God is left out, inadequate answers to life's biggest questions invariably lead to individual and social problems.

Alexander Solzhenitsyn, the Russian writer who escaped persecution in the former Soviet Union by fleeing to the United States, observed that in the West, individual human rights had finally been achieved, but not without cost. In a Harvard University commencement address in 1978, delivered shortly after his exile to America, Solzhenitsyn identified America's problem as "the proclaimed and enforced autonomy of man from any higher force above him. It could also be called anthropocentricity, with man seen as the center of everything that exists." He warned of the "dangerous trend to worship man and his material needs.... In early democracies, as in the American democracy at the time of its birth, all individual human rights were granted because man is God's creature ... but man's sense of responsibility to God and society grew dimmer and dimmer" (1978).

Solzhenitsyn's words, spoken nearly four decades ago, have proven prophetic. In the prevailing cultural worldview today, human beings are central, not God, and the danger is the worship of man and material needs.

Christian schools should be different, and that difference is a function of the strategic design of the curriculum. We should never find so little difference between secular and Christian schools that one might call to merge the two systems as Holland did. Carrying out that distinctive through the curriculum is the subject of later chapters.

Why Integration Is a Necessity

It would be nice if children were blank tablets on which to be written. We could "write" biblical answers to life's biggest questions, give a test, and see if each could answer the basic questions of life. But worldviews are messy. They begin to develop very early in an infant's life. When children begin formal education, they already have a forming worldview. Older children and teens may even a somewhat developed worldview.

This is why a worldview must be integrated into *all* aspects of the school. Students must learn to distinguish a Christian worldview from other worldviews. They need Scripture to *inform* their worldviews and *reform* their minds. The ultimate goal of worldview integration is a biblically *formed* worldview that will stand the tests of life. But it is the process of a lifetime!

ACTIVITY

Write a position paper in which you defend biblical worldview integration in the design of the school curriculum as though you were presenting it to the faculty of your school.

Five

Cultural Barriers to the Development of a Truly Christian Worldview

The alternative worldviews being promoted in media and educational materials present a major barrier to the development of a Christian worldview. The most prominent worldview, naturalism, encourages dualistic thinking, one of the major barriers to developing a Christian worldview. Another problematic worldview, Westernized pantheism, encourages a second barrier: pluralistic thinking, which posits that all beliefs can be true. In an increasingly narcissistic culture, this worldview is gaining ground fast.

Naturalism and Divided Worldviews

Naturalism has dominated academia for many years. It reduces the world and life to material, places its faith in science, and labels spirituality an invention of the human brain for survival. This tacit acknowledgement of spiritual beliefs, however, has opened the door for worldview duplicity. Scholars who hold to any worldview other than naturalism must live out of a divided worldview, leaving their "private" beliefs at the door when they come to study or work. To the philosophical naturalist, religion and most other worldviews belong to the domain of private values or feelings, while science is the domain of the intellect. Naturalism becomes the only "acceptable" worldview of the thinking man or woman, and so any scholar who holds other beliefs must live out of a divided worldview.

Abraham Kuyper recognized this first barrier to the development of a biblically-based worldview when he spoke about education at the Free University of Amsterdam. In his address, Kuyper hinted at the negative consequences of allowing academic disciplines to have sovereignty in their own sphere without submitting to a higher authority. For Kuyper, this supreme authority was Christ. When individual disciplines or domains take on supreme sovereignty, they are allowed to "swallow all other Sovereignties" such as conscience, family, pedagogy, and spirituality. Prior to and during Kuyper's lifetime, the higher authority that had kept the domains of scholarship within their own boundaries was the state. The newly established Free University of Amsterdam was to be one in which students were free to study all domains of inquiry under the supreme authority of God. Kuyper's main thesis was given in his most frequently quoted words: "There is not a square inch in the whole domain of our human existence over which Christ, Who is Sovereign over all, does not cry: 'Mine!'" Kuyper viewed all of life and learning under the authority of Scripture.

One hundred years after Kuyper's address, three sociologists at the University of Texas at Arlington conducted research to determine why students coming to their university right out of high school respected "the prestige and authority of science" but held to beliefs that contradicted the researchers' scientific system of thinking. The authors reported that those who believed in God, creation, the Bible, UFOs, parapsychology, séances, past lives, and the like were classified as mentally deficient. "In the old days ... [social scientists] diagnosed symptoms, declared the subject mentally ill, and prescribed cures" (Taylor, Eve, and Harrold 1995). The researchers strove to understand students whose worldviews conflicted with those of the researchers.

They administered a questionnaire to gauge students' beliefs in a wide variety of "pseudoscientific" concepts (Bigfoot, UFOs, psychic powers, and aliens from outer space appeared alongside Noah's ark, creation, and Adam and Eve as literal people) as well as widely accepted scientific concepts. This yielded three distinct groups:

Cultural Traditionalists

Members of this group "believed a thing to be true because of faith, tradition, revelation, or authority. Such an attitude might be summed up in bumper sticker declarations such as 'God said it, I believe it, that settles it.'"

Cultural Modernists

Members of this group hold that truth can be found by evaluating hypotheses on the basis of empirical testing. It stresses empiricism and scientific inquiry. (The researchers placed themselves in this camp.)

Cultural Postmodernists

An emerging subculture among the three groups, cultural postmodernism opposes both cultural traditionalism and cultural modernism. Members of the group view modernism "as having led to rampant militarism, consumerism, pollution, and global warming." Members of this group believe "an adequate explanation requires other forms of spirituality" and that "pagan religions from previous times have much to teach us about how to solve today's problems."

The researchers concluded that each of the three worldviews uses a different set of "rules for knowing" to determine truth. They went on to argue that spiritual beliefs spring from these rules, not from ignorance, stupidity, or a disorder. (Nice to know!)

The last conclusion intrigued me the most. After declaring that debunking other worldviews of students coming to their university campus was not the best approach, they concluded:

> Is it possible that one might use cultural traditionalist rules when considering the origins of humanity when one is in the traditional religious community, but unknowingly switch to a different set of rules for knowing when one arrives on a college or university campus and is asked to understand molecular biology? Do people use one set of rules for knowing when they are on campus and another when they return to a traditional community?

These concluding questions imply that it is just fine for students to use pseudoscientific beliefs in their religious community but use a different set of rules for knowing in an academic context. This is a tacit approval of worldview duplicity!

The danger that was apparent in Kuyper's day was that one domain of human life could take over in the academic life of humanity as supreme. That danger is deeply embedded in academic institutions today. This kind of thinking is not only present in higher education but in all levels of basic education as well. "Inferior" religious beliefs are acceptable in private and in home communities for weddings, funerals, and holidays, but not acceptable in the classroom!

The First Barrier: A Divided Worldview

The division of the sacred and the secular has become a barrier to developing a biblical worldview. Some Christian institutions perpetuate this duplicity by adding a "spiritual" component—chapel, Bible class, prayers before the lesson—to a functionally secular curriculum. Christian schools cannot allow this kind of thinking to survive among their faculty.

This sacred/secular division has impacted education as much or more than any other issue in our time. It has led to destructive consequences—and not only for Christians! Contemporary educators have acknowledged the need for integrity in life. Integrity is the result of having an integrated mind and life—of being the same person at home, at church, in community, and in the classroom.

Yale professor Steven Carter wrote in *Culture of Disbelief*:

> We often ask our citizens to split their public and private selves, telling them in effect that it is fine to be religious in private, but there is something askew when those private beliefs become the basis for public action. (1993)

A thought-life dichotomy leads to personality disintegration! A divided worldview impacts Christians in the church, the school, the work place—in all of life! The divide presents a barrier to true curricular biblical integration.

In the next chapter we will look at naturalism as a worldview and demonstrate how to connect the knowledge available in the sciences with a biblical view of the natural world. While naturalists or materialists may be at odds with the Bible, science and the Bible are not at odds with each other.

The Second Barrier: Pluralism

With the globalization of media, pluralism has made inroads into broad geographical cultures that were, until recently, homogeneous. Though there are many benefits to pluralism and diversity, there is also a great danger, as Ravi Zacharias identified in *Deliver Us From Evil*.

> The great glory and strength of pluralism is that it compels the holder of any belief to measure its truthfulness against alternative interpretations. The great hazard of pluralism is the faulty deduction, in the name of tolerance, that all beliefs can be equally true. It is ultimately truth, not popularity or rights that determines destiny. (1996)

Pluralism even functions as a quasi-worldview. In an interview, actress Sarah Michelle Gellar-Prinze said of her basic beliefs:

> I consider myself a spiritual person. I believe in an idea of God, although it's my own personal ideal. I find most religions interesting, and I've been to every kind of denomination: Catholic, Christian, Jewish, Buddhist. I've taken bits and pieces from everything and customized it. (Olsen 2002)

Gellar-Prinze has become her own measure for truth: she has her own idea of God, and has "taken bits and pieces from everything and customized it." The standard for truth is not science, God, or, indeed, any standard outside her own thoughts. Instead, she turns to a pluralism that can include anything, even if the beliefs contradict one another.

The same type of thinking forms the central theme of *The Life of Pi* by Yann Martel. In the book, Piscine "Pi" Patel escapes a devastating shipwreck aboard a lifeboat. His companions are surviving zoo animals: an orangutan, a hyena, a zebra, and a Bengal tiger. Before long, only Pi and the tiger remain, and together they endure a 227-day voyage toward land. After landing on the shore of Mexico, Pi recounts his story to two men from the Maritime Department. They don't believe him, so he changes the characters from animals to humans— his mother, the cook, a young Taiwanese soldier—that parallel the animal story.

Which story is true? According to Pi, it doesn't really matter. Pi says, "I told you two stories.... Neither makes a factual difference to you. You can't prove which story is true and which is not. You must take my word for it." Neither story explains why the ship sank. Pi asks the two men which story they preferred. They choose the animal story, and Pi replies, "And so it goes with God."

This is the culmination of the book's themes. Though born into a Hindu family, Pi claims to be an adherent to *three* separate faiths: the Hinduism of his family, Christianity, and Islam. But the center of authority for Pi's worldview resides within Pi himself—he selects the elements from each tradition that he thinks make for a better story. Pi's faith conflicts with Christ's claim to be "*the* way, *the* truth, and *the* life," but fits neatly with the Bhagavad Gita, in which God states that "As people approach me, so I receive them. All paths lead to me."

Pi's beliefs are ultimately his preferences. Pi becomes his own measure for truth. His story exposes a war between the mind and the heart, and Pi chooses the heart.

We are living at a time when the heart is more important than the mind to many. Is this a biblical view or a false dichotomy? Does God bypass the mind to get to the heart? No! We are instructed to love the Lord with *all* our heart, soul, and mind. Love for God includes our whole being as a unit.

A Heart/Mind Dichotomy

Pluralistic and postmodern thinking have impacted our culture. Sadly, even many Christians hold a "Christian" worldview that is devoid of biblical content. Pluralism has become a barrier to biblical thinking. The Christian worldview is, in some cases, chosen by default: a person may think, "I am not a Muslim, a Jew, a Hindu, or a Buddhist, and I do believe in a higher power of some kind, so I guess I am a Christian" or "I was born Christian, so I guess I am Christian. But there are many different roads to God." This kind of thinking is the reason why it is distinctive to use the term *biblical* worldview or *biblical* Christian worldview.

Whether it is naturalism, which has led to an academic/personal divide, or worldview pluralism with its worship of subjectivity, barriers to biblical worldview integration must be overcome in the Christian community. Integration, and the integrity that should follow, are vital to the Christian walk.

"The *integrity* of the upright guides them, but the unfaithful are destroyed by their duplicity."

—Proverbs 11:3

"Teach me your way, O Lord, that I may rely on your faithfulness; give me an *undivided heart*, that I may fear your name. I will praise you, O Lord my God, with all my heart; I will glorify your name forever."

—Psalm 86:11

ACTIVITY

If one of the cultural barriers addressed in this chapter were operating in the culture of your school right now, how would you combat it? Name the barrier and create the strategy. Share it with your colleagues with a defense of why it is important to tear down the barrier.

Six

Naturalism

The primary focus of this book is not to present and critique various worldviews; however, a degree of familiarity with contemporary worldviews is necessary in developing the kind of thinking that is essential in developing a truly integrated curriculum. The presentation and illustrations of three broad worldviews in the next few chapters will, I hope, help readers to evaluate curriculum materials with an eye toward identifying underlying beliefs. The goal is not necessarily to identify the specific tenets of each worldview, but to increase general awareness, especially of how each worldview differs from Christianity. A disposition toward worldview thinking is vital in the ongoing development of biblical integration.

Those who are serious about biblical integration can study various worldviews in greater depth through the numerous excellent books on the subjects (I have used the broad overviews in *The Universe Next Door* for many years).

Practicing Worldview Thinking

Every worldview attempts to answer the fundamental questions of life. These questions often fall into one of the following three categories.

Metaphysics—What is ultimate reality?

Why is there something rather than nothing? What is really real? Does God exist? What kind of God? What is God's role, if any, in human affairs? What is the nature of human beings? What is the nature and source of the external world? How do God, humans, and the universe relate, if at all?

Epistemology—How do we come to know?

Is knowledge subjective or objective, relative or absolute? Is it objective but understood with a measure of subjectivity? What is the nature of knowledge and knowing? Is there knowledge outside the human mind or do we create it with the mind? Can we truly know anything?

Axiology—What is of value?

How do we determine the good and the beautiful (ethics and aesthetics)? What are right values and right actions? Do both good and evil exist in the world, and if so, why? What is the answer to the problem of evil (hate, crime, wars, etc.) in the world?

This chapter will deal with how naturalism responds to worldview questions; the following two chapters will address Eastern pantheism and naturalistic pantheism. Other worldviews will be mentioned briefly as well.

Naturalism: What Is It?

Naturalism has come in many variations: scientific naturalism, atheistic naturalism, scientism, materialism, religious naturalism, and secular humanism. Religious naturalism and secular humanism are unique among the others in their efforts to salvage the human being from the dehumanizing conclusions of the naturalistic worldview. This can be seen clearly in the 1933, 1973, and 2003 versions of the Humanist Manifesto.

Each of the three versions of the Humanist Manifesto reflects a developing worldview that is at the core naturalistic, but attempts to project a more prominent place for the human being than pure naturalism allows. During the twentieth century, secular humanism became the leading voice for naturalism in the United States. Changes in cultural views over time have served to modify the language of the stated beliefs, but each document denies a supernatural God and adheres to naturalism as a worldview.

Roy Wood Sellars, who drafted the initial text of the Humanist Manifesto, admitted in an article in *The New Humanist* that secular humanism is "in many ways diametrically opposed to the fundamentals accepted by Christianity." Humanism regards "even the minimum theistic fundamentals" untenable; they consider naturalism and theism mutually exclusive. Near the end of the article, Sellars wrote, "We may define religious humanism accordingly as religion adjusted to an intelligent naturalism" (1933).

What do naturalistic humanists believe? According to the 1933 Humanist Manifesto, they "regard the universe as self-existing and not created" and hold "that man is a part of nature and that he has emerged as the result of a continuous process." The fifth and sixth belief statements of the original document state, "The nature of the universe depicted by modern science makes unacceptable any supernatural or cosmic guarantees of human values.... We are convinced that the time has passed for theism, deism, modernism, and the several varieties of 'new thought.'" The final paragraph insists that man alone is the central figure in obtaining meaning: "Man is at last becoming aware that he alone is responsible for the realization of the world of his dreams, that *he has within himself* the power for its achievement" (emphasis added). Clearly, there is no place for God in this worldview; the human as a part of nature has become the focal point.

Why "Humanism"?

Sellars explains, "We adopted the term humanism because it was, quite obviously, the one suitable term. Reject theism as the logical center of religion and the only alternative is to take man as the center. The new religion is homocentric and not theo-centric" (1933).

These beliefs did not change with later revisions to the manifesto. In 2000, the late Paul Kurtz, "father of secular humanism," issued a call for planetary humanism. Kurtz offered a *post*-postmodern humanism that was optimistic about humankind's ability to solve all problems by rational means. He reiterated the exhortation that "humans not look beyond themselves for salvation. We alone are responsible for our own destiny."

Kurtz went on to confirm that, "The unique message of humanism on the current world scene is its commitment to scientific naturalism. Most worldviews accepted today are spiritual, mystical, or theological in character.... Scientific naturalism enables human beings to construct a coherent worldview disentangled from metaphysics or theology and based on the sciences."

While Kurtz calls for toleration of "cultural diversity except where those cultures are intolerant or repressive," he also believed that "parents should not simply impose their own religious outlook or moral values on their children or indoctrinate them." The great fear in the last quarter of the twentieth century was that scientific humanism, because of its claim to be rational and neutral, would be taught in schools and acceptable in public education and the beliefs of parents would be ridiculed, encouraging students to "come on board" with scientific humanism. Many Christian schools were propelled into existence in the 1970s to challenge this cultural invasion, but this did nothing to halt the integration of public schools around secular humanism. Naturalism, not neutrality, had won the day.

Long Before a Naturalistic Manifesto

The birth of scientific naturalism preceded the written manifestos by many years. In fact, it began to emerge during the Enlightenment period in the seventeenth and eighteenth centuries.

It appeared in the writings of Karl Marx and Friedrich Engels in the nineteenth century; it entered an optimistic American culture during the early part of the twentieth century.

Humanism ran counter to the negative mood that naturalism had brought on in Europe. Naturalism views humans as specks of cosmic dust, living on Earth by chance and without purpose. It opposes the desire to frame humans as important figures in the vastness of nature. Secular humanism placed humankind at the helm of a cold and unfeeling universe. Humans are the central focus of the cosmos because of our reasoning capacity. As they declared in the 1973 iteration of the Humanist Manifesto:

> As nontheists, we begin with humans, not God, nature not deity.... We can discover no divine purpose or providence for the human species.... Humans are responsible for what we are or will become. No deity will save us; we must save ourselves.... Thus engaged in the flow of life, we aspire to this vision with the informed conviction that humanity has the ability to progress toward its highest ideals. The responsibility for our lives and the kind of world in which we live is ours and ours alone.

Earlier forms of naturalistic philosophy have been criticized for being dehumanizing. Naturalism demoted humans to beings determined by the blind mechanisms of cause and effect—there was no free will or choice. This is the logical conclusion of pure naturalism. But many humans could not tolerate such a cold worldview. The manifestoes presented an attractively optimistic version of naturalism. The human became the foundational starting point for the worldview in spite of the logical conclusion of scientific naturalism.

In *Idols for Destructions*, historian Herbert Schlossberg declares, "Humanism is fundamentally irrational. Although naturalistic in most of its forms, it nevertheless professes belief in the special worth and dignity of human beings, a position for which there can be no support in naturalism" (1983).

Basic Beliefs of Naturalism

Metaphysics: Issues of Existence	The source of all that exists is *matter;* one reality exists and it is material; there is no spirit, no immaterial part; there is no God.
	The cosmos is all there is, was, or ever will be; nature is in its normal, natural state.
	Humans are material only (no intrinsic nature, purpose, or soul) specially evolved in intellect and language.
	No life after physical death—only decomposed matter; focus on the here and now.
Epistemology: Issues of Knowing	Humans know truth through their senses *only;* God cannot be known through the senses, therefore talk of God is *nonsense.*
	Truth can be found only through empirical evidence, intellect, and the mechanisms of science.
Axiology: Issues of Valuing	Values are "born out of the human experiment," hardwired by genetics, or conditioned by the environment.
	Life is a human experiment.

Identifying Naturalism in School Curricula

The following quotes and curricular examples are meant to illustrate naturalistic thinking and to encourage teachers to develop a disposition toward worldview thinking. In each case, one might ask what does and does not fit with a Christian worldview. This is the core of worldview thinking.

"Blind, Pitiless Indifference"

Richard Dawkins, one of the leading proponents of atheistic naturalism today, summarized his beliefs in an article written for *Scientific American.*

> In a universe of electrons and selfish genes, blind physical forces and genetic replication, some people are going to get hurt, other people are going to get lucky, and you won't find any rhyme or reason in it, nor any justice. The universe that we observe has precisely the properties we should expect if there is, at bottom, no design, no purpose, no evil, no good, nothing but pitiless indifference. As that unhappy poet, A.E. Housman put it, "For Nature, heartless, witless nature / Will neither care nor know." DNA neither cares nor knows. DNA just is. And we dance to its music. (1995; emphasis added)

In just one brief paragraph, Dawkins addresses several worldview answers held by atheistic naturalists. What is the nature of the external world? *A lucky happening!* There is no design, no purpose, and no designer. What is a human being? Genetic stuff; we are slaves to DNA. Life circumstances are a matter of *luck!* How do we know right and wrong? There is neither evil nor good.

"The Result Only of Chance"

The concept of luck is not uncommon among naturalists. David Waltham, scientist in the department of earth sciences at Royal Holloway College at the University of London and author of *Lucky Planet*, wrote:

> The gradually increasing heat from our Sun has been consistently countered by decreasing greenhouse-gas concentrations, and Earth has cooled slightly through time instead of warming up. Those falling temperatures are quite mysterious since natural climate-control mechanisms might have reduced the effects of solar warming but cannot have reversed them to produce a cooling. Earth's relatively stable climatic history can therefore be the result only of chance.

> To me, that is the most convincing evidence available that good fortune played a leading role in the success of life here. Think about it: a spot in the universe where life got started, where environmental conditions were continuously life-friendly, and where evolution happened to follow the path to self-awareness. In a universe of innumerable possibilities, how often will that particular route be followed? (2014)

No wonder naturalists cling to the concept of luck. The improbability of life on a planet in our universe is astronomical! And yet the earth supports life. If there is no God, no design or purpose, only luck could be responsible for this good outcome. This is the logical conclusion of their worldview. This view of Earth is presented in several textbooks.

How might we respond in a Christian educational setting without doing an injustice to the science of the earth and without fragmenting learning? That is, how might we practice worldview integration in the curriculum? When we encounter science textbooks which acknowledge how perfect Earth is for life, but attribute this suitability to *luck*, how should we address it?

First, we must understand biblical worldview integration as a process of *connecting* and *distinguishing*. There are wonderful opportunities to connect academic content to God's perspective. When we discuss the suitability of Earth for human life, we must help our students understand that the concept is compatible both with God's Word—His direct revelation to us—

and with what we learn through science. Science helps us to see that Earth provides everything necessary for life. Isaiah 45:18 says, "He who created the heavens, he is God; he who fashioned and made the earth, he founded it; he did not create it to be empty, *he formed it to be inhabited.*"

The very habitation of the earth by humans living on this planet is a testimony to God's power and divine nature, so much so that we are without excuse if we do not believe in God's existence. Those who do not believe "exchange the truth of God for a lie." (Romans 1:25). Giving God credit for His work in creation is the simplest form of worship in science class.

The extraordinary characteristics of the earth should cause humans to reach out to the God of the universe. Science is not in conflict with a Christian worldview. Science, as the study of the natural world, is not the domain of the naturalist alone; many scientists are Christians and do their work for God's glory. This is God's world; He created it and has given humankind the capacity to study it and use it.

The integration of a Christian worldview brings together what science has discovered with biblical truth.

But this curricular integration must be preceded by the teacher's own process of biblical integration. In the curriculum, integration is accomplished by the creation of student activities that are infused directly into the regular lesson plan. A teacher will ask herself, "What student activity might cause the students to *connect* the suitability of Earth for life to the intelligence of a Creator rather than just the luck of the cosmos?" What in the text or lesson must be distinguished from a Christian worldview?

The naturalist would say, "Aren't we lucky that our planet is so well suited for life!" This answer will be reflected in countless textbooks. But if our students think *in science class* that our planet's habitability is due to the luck of the cosmos, and think *in Bible class* that we owe our very breath to God, what might this divided thinking do to their worldview development?

"We, Too, Must Be Cruel"

> "Nature is cruel: therefore, we, too, must be cruel. If I can send the flower of the German nation into the hell of war without the smallest pity for the spilling of precious German blood, then surely I have the right to remove millions of an inferior race that breeds like vermin."   —Adolf Hitler

Whether the quote is actually spoken by Hitler has been debated, but Hitler's worldview was arguably naturalistic and his intention to depopulate Germany of Jews and gypsies is not questioned. He believed in, and sought to guide, naturalistic determinism. Race was the evolutionary category to purify humankind. The eradication of certain "inferior" races was his goal.

Why would Hitler demonstrate so little regard for human life? He was drawing logical conclusions and acting upon his worldview. He was accelerating natural selection: eliminating a weak race to favor a strong one.

Naturalism holds that humans, having evolved reason, can now, to some degree, control their own evolution. Once a process controlled by chance mutations and luck, natural selection can now be guided by human hands; we can perfect our own evolution. This fits very neatly with Hitler's goal.

There are plenty of naturalists who did and do condemn Hitler. B.F. Skinner, for example, wanted to produce a good society by conditioning people to behave well. But his envisioned utopia is rather chilling: for if humankind is flawed and must be trained, who trains the trainer? Who would decide the values needed to condition humans in the society and on what basis?

No Soul! No Mind!

Words like "soul" or "mind," as things separate from the physical brain, had no place at all in a naturalistic worldview. There was no spirit; there was no spiritual realm; there was no spiritual God. Friedrich Nietzsche famously concluded that "God is dead!" But naturalism did not only kill God; it dehumanized humans, killed personhood, and eventually led to nihilism, a worldview that denies any objective ground for truth, especially moral truths. It disregarded traditional values and beliefs, including any value in human personhood; after all, what transcendent entity gives us value? To the nihilist, existence is senseless and useless. There is no intrinsic worth and no designed purpose for human beings; humans just exist.

The promises of naturalism fell under scrutiny in the West at the end of World War II, after the bombing of Hiroshima and Nagasaki. Twenty-five percent of the population of the two cities died. Many more were burned and sickened. This was what science had wrought. The hope that science could usher in a utopia began to wane.

It is no wonder that the idea of humans as "gods" entered the Western world through Eastern pantheism, the increasingly popular worldview addressed in the next chapter. The human heart cries, "We have worth, don't we?" This was the question asked by atheistic naturalists seeking meaning in life. Humanism offered the belief that, though we are just a material speck in the cosmos, we are not simply determined by the environment; we can choose and make ourselves. But even this thought did not satisfy the human heart. We were ripe for the entrance of Eastern mysticism.

"What Many People Think of as Free Will"

Many naturalists, though not all, hold to the logical conclusions of naturalistic determinism, the belief that all events are caused by external factors. The human is therefore not a responsible moral agent.

> We do not have what many people think of as free will, being able to cause our behavior without our being fully caused in turn.... Therefore individuals don't bear ultimate originative responsibility for their actions, in the sense of being their first cause. Given the circumstances both inside and outside the body they couldn't have done other than what they did.... Naturalism does call into question the basis for retributive attitudes, namely the idea that individuals could have done otherwise in the situation in which their behavior arose and so deeply deserve punishment. (www.naturalism.org/worldview-naturalism/tenets-of-naturalism)

This endorsement of victimhood, the thinking that nothing is "my fault," is one possible implication of the moral code birthed out of naturalism. Humans are hardwired by evolutionary processes or conditioned by the environment. We are victims of inscrutable external forces, reducing or entirely removing personal moral responsibility. There is "no evil, no good." According to the same naturalistic tenets:

> We need not appeal to a supernatural standard of ethical conduct to know that in general it's wrong to lie, cheat, steal, rape, murder, torture, or otherwise treat people in ways we'd rather not be treated. Our naturally endowed empathetic concern for others and our hardwired penchant for cooperation and reciprocity get us what we most want as social creatures: to flourish as individuals within a community.

Our experience tells us otherwise. Humans need outside intervention and help in overcoming the results of a fallen nature. While we can do good deeds and care for others, we are prone to self-centeredness and bad moral choices. Nature has not endowed us with a standard for ethical choices and behaviors. The only reasonable standard for ethics is God's character.

Naturalism in Education

Some science curricula today recommend using reruns of the Discovery Channel's popular 1980 TV program, *Cosmos,* hosted by Carl Sagan. Sagan, a self-proclaimed atheistic naturalist, never gives God credit for His creatorship. God is not his starting point or foundational belief in determining ultimate reality. Sagan opened the *Cosmos* with his trademark statement: "The cosmos is all that is, or ever was, or ever will be."

This thought process can be found in some unexpected places. For 30 years, I lived in the county where Stan and Jan Berenstain, authors of the popular *Berenstain Bears* series, lived and worked. I have enjoyed their books for many years. It was with some surprise that I discovered that right in the middle of *The Berenstain Bears' Big Book of Science and Nature*, the question, "What is Nature?" was answered, "It's everybody and everything ... Nature is you! Nature is me! It's all that is or was or ever will be!"

Some parents and teachers may unwittingly read this page with kids without distinguishing the comment from a biblical view. But it is crucial for Christian educators and parents to *distinguish* this perspective from a Christian view of nature. This does not mean censoring the book itself; children need to know that some people do not hold the same beliefs that we do as Christians.

In spite of the issue above, there is much in the book to *connect* with God as the designer and Creator of the world around us. I would use the *Big Book of Science and Nature* in a classroom. The first step is thinking critically about the material. If there is an opportunity to biblically integrate the material—either by comparing and contrasting or connecting and distinguishing—I would plan to do so. The statement that nature is "all that is, or was, or ever will be" must be challenged so that the concept can be distinguished from a Christian view of creation. The distinguishing process helps to fortify the developing Christian worldview.

Some parents and teachers might assume that the book needs no critical analysis. I found the book advertised on Christianbook.com, an endorsement which may imply to some Christian educators that there is nothing in the book about which to be concerned. I have also found several primary level teachers and some homeschooling parents who commented that they use the book to supplement their curriculum materials.

How could a teacher integrate a biblical worldview with this book? One activity might be to have children think of ways to change the saying in the book to one that fits God's perspective. Read Revelation 4:8b: "Holy, holy, holy is the Lord God Almighty, who was, and is, and is to come." Then read Revelation 22:13: "I am the Alpha and the Omega, the First and the Last, the Beginning and the End." Tell the students about the Greek alphabet, which begins with *alpha* and ends with *omega*; God is the beginning and the end. This *distinguishes* the Christian worldview. To *connect* the Christian worldview with the book, a teacher might create an activity that includes the biblical view that God created all the wonderful things in nature: animals, plants, seasons, and us.

Many more opportunities for worldview integration may be found in everyday life, media, books, and curriculum materials. Developing a worldview perspective and the habit of identifying opportunities is crucial for any educator, for while worldview integration begins with the teacher's own integrative thinking, student activities are what guide students to process concepts that fit with a biblical worldview and distinguish the things that do not fit.

ACTIVITY

Scan a set of curriculum materials for your grade level and try to identify naturalistic assumptions implying that there is no God, no absolute moral standard, little or no moral responsibility, or that knowledge cannot be obtained except through science. This is a distinction process.

Scan your curriculum materials and try to identify topics and subject areas that clearly correlate with the foundational belief that God exists (even if God is not mentioned), is intelligent, is powerful in sustaining life, is creative, etc. Cite places where humans invent, create, communicate, express emotions, etc. Plan to connect these to a biblical worldview; humans bear the image of God and have inherent value.

Seven

Pantheism

Dissatisfaction with Naturalism

In the late 1960s and early 70s, the American youth rejected the harsh realities of war. They attributed these "insane human behaviors" to a worldview that viewed humans as a part of evolved matter, specks of cosmic dust without soul or feelings. Some went so far as to reject reason, science, and even technology, for their connection to the "modern world." Naturalism had ushered in meaninglessness; humans are nothing more than sophisticated machines with no design, purpose, or free will to choose. The conclusion that we are alone in the universe was a scary thought. Naturalism had promised a utopia, but instead led to meaninglessness, dehumanization, and war. Traditional beliefs, including theism, were widely scorned, especially in academic circles. Where were the youth of that day to turn?

John Osborne's *The Entertainer*, a three-act play written during this tumultuous period, reveals the prevailing view of turning to the self for meaning in the character, Jean, who says:

> Here we are, we're alone in the universe, there's no God, it just seems that it all began by something as simple as sunlight striking on a piece of rock. And here we are. We've only got ourselves. Somehow, we've just got to make a go of it. We've only ourselves. (1957)

The solution for human meaninglessness was to focus life on human choice; that which could "make the person" and give some measure of meaning to existence. Theirs was an attempt to salvage the human being from hardline naturalism and its resultant cold determinism. "We are not products of deterministic nature alone," they declared. "We have value! We can choose!" Atheistic existentialism concluded that we make our nature or our "essence." It was Jean Paul Sartre who succinctly declared, "Existence precedes essence." To the existentialists, humans possess no innate nature. We make ourselves by our choices.

The logical conclusion of naturalism seemed to be despair, apathy, or acceptance of an "absurd" life. Albert Camus, for example, dissociated himself from the pessimistic existentialists while still acknowledging man's lonely condition in the universe. His "man of the absurd" rejects despair, instead committing himself to the responsibility of living as best he can. In his 1961 collection of essays, *Resistance, Rebellion and Death*, Camus wrote: "I continue to believe that this world has no ultimate meaning. But I know that something in it has a meaning and that is man, because he is the only creature to insist on having one." Humankind had become the center of his worldview. Human subjective thoughts and feelings were of equal value with the objective sciences.

> In existentialism, the individual's starting point is characterized by what has been called "the existential attitude" or a sense of disorientation and confusion in the face of an apparently meaningless or absurd world. (Solomon, 1974)

Theism would have served as a better alternative to cold naturalism, but its foundational belief in God was now "outdated" and out of the question for many. The ultimate reality of the naturalists, nihilists, and atheistic existentialists was matter and nothing else. Jean-Paul Sartre put it this way:

> The existentialist ... thinks it very distressing that God does not exist, because all possibility of finding values in a heaven of ideas disappears along with Him; there can no longer be an *a priori* Good, since there is no infinite and perfect consciousness to think it. Nowhere is it written that the Good exists, that we must be honest, that we must not lie; because the fact is we are on a plane where there are only men. Dostoyevsky said, "If God didn't exist, everything would be permissible." That is the very starting point of existentialism. Indeed, everything is permissible if God does not exist, and as a result, man is forlorn, because neither within him nor without does he find anything to cling to. (1993, *Essays in Existentialism*)

Notice Sartre's conclusion that there is nothing the human being can cling to, inside themselves or outside. Not even nature's development of the human brain and reason could come to the rescue.

Existentialism became widespread in North America in the 1960s, seeping into the culture by way of the arts; literature classes often dealt with poetry and novels written by existentialists. But existentialist thinking did not completely satisfy the young adults of the late 1960s and early 1970s. "Making myself" by my choices, my own creativity, and my actions led to gaining worth through my performance and projects—an unacceptable thought to students who loved the "freedom" and "choice" part of existentialism.

I wrote my master's thesis during this time period, studying teens. The youth of the day were restless and bohemian, experimenting with the drug culture and communal living. They rejected war and the values of the middle class, and saw naturalism in any of its forms as a challenge to human relationships and worth. A new shift in worldview thinking was on the horizon in the West. It was a new day! The hope was to salvage the worth of human beings.

A New Age Worldview Shift

American youth were ready for a new view of the world and life. Mama Cass, with her wonderful robust voice, stood on stage and was seen on TV singing:

There's a new world coming　　　　　　*There's a brand new morning*
And it's just around the bend　　　　　　*Rising clear and sweet and free*
There's a new world coming　　　　　　*There's a new day dawning*
This one's coming to an end　　　　　　*That belongs to you and me.*

There's a new voice calling　　　　　　*Yes a new world's coming*
You can hear it if you try　　　　　　*The one we've had visions of*
And it's growing stronger　　　　　　*Coming in peace, coming in joy*
With each day that passes by　　　　　　*Coming in love*

If life was to be engaged as the optimistic existentialist believed, then our personal choices will make a new world. This was fertile ground for an even more inward focus; the West was ready to meet the East in an emerging worldview.

The New Westernized Pantheism

Eastern pantheism had already been around for hundreds of years before it entered Western vocabulary as "pantheism." It was popularized in the seventeenth century by Dutch philosopher Baruch Spinoza, who was attempting to describe monism, the concept that everything, including God, is of one substance. Spinoza's form of pantheism was not appreciated by his Jewish community nor by the Catholic church, both of which held that God is transcendent and is completely other than the universe.

Pantheistic ideas gained ground in the nineteenth century, flowering in the works of several novelists and poets who had encountered pantheistic ideas firsthand. The Westernized version in the twentieth century led to the New Age movement, a popular worldview among young people of the 1970s.

One of my first encounters with Eastern thinking was in a college class studying major religions of the world. The views of Hinduism and Buddhism were representative of pantheistic thought (although there are major differences). The following chart selects some of the beliefs that, in general, represent pantheistic thought.

Eastern Pantheism

Metaphysics: Issues of Existence	Ultimate reality is *impersonal* energy or non-material; the "One." The universe flows out of the One and the One is the universe. This is a monistic view. "Brahman" is the ultimate reality in the major expression of Hinduism; some groups of Hindus believe in many gods that have emanated from the One. (Buddhism does not accept a divine agency or creative agency.) Humans are part of the One; therefore, humans are god. This is typified in the statement "*atman* is *Brahman*," meaning the soul of the human is the soul of the cosmos. All creatures pass through cycles of birth, death, and reincarnation. The ultimate goal is Nirvana, to be one with the impersonal All; all paths lead to this goal, where personhood and individuality cease to be.
Epistemology: Issues of Knowing	Humans know "truth" through personal experience and do not appeal to logic; apparent differences and distinctions are not real; no real distinction between truth and falsehood. Method for truth-judging is personal, numinous, and intuitive; higher knowledge (higher states of consciousness) is championed over "lower" scientific knowledge. Being trumps knowing.
Axiology: Issues of Valuing	Values are what one decides as an individual; good and evil are products of duality, which is an illusion. Turn inward, trust your heart; you are god, and can trust yourself. Good and bad are illusions with which the enlightened person need not be concerned; good and bad will be balanced when the "true self" is reached through enlightenment. Helping those of lower status conflicts with their punishment for bad karma; some hold that helping another is only good for the person who is helping.

A Turning Point in Worldview Thinking

President Nixon's inaugural address came on the heels of the Vietnam War. Science was still claiming utopian hope in humanity, but had not yet achieved its most visible victory—the moon landing. The crisis of the day, according to Nixon, was not technological advancement, but a crisis of the spirit of humankind.

> To a crisis of the spirit, we need an answer of the spirit. To find that answer, we need only look *within ourselves*.... In that moment of surpassing technological triumph, men turned their thoughts toward home and humanity—seeing in that far perspective that man's destiny on Earth is not divisible; telling us that however far we reach into the cosmos, our destiny lies not in the stars but on *Earth itself, in our own hands, in our own hearts*. We have endured a long night of the American spirit. But as our eyes catch the dimness of the first rays of dawn, let us not curse the remaining dark. Let us gather the light. Our destiny offers *not the cup of despair*, but the chalice of opportunity." (1969; emphasis added).

In the rhetoric itself, one can see some of the influences of emerging pantheism. The prevailing worldview of naturalism and its younger sibling, optimistic existentialism, were about to come into conflict with a worldview that declared the "human spirit" was more than matter, that there is something to cling to inside us, if we only turn within!

Eastern Pantheism's Answers to Worldview Questions

Pantheism places little stock in empirically testable factors, preferring to turn inward to the "god" inside. The answer to human problems is not science, nor our simple humanity; we are part of god. Therefore, we can turn inward to change ourselves and the world. Stephen Prothero concluded that in Hindu belief, "You will see that you too are divine. Our sense of separateness from God is but a shadow cast on the wall of the cave. The sacred is inside us. The essence of the human being is the same as the essence of divinity" (2010). We are not biological machines or absurdist creatures; we have an essence, and it is god.

According to Deepak Chopra, an Indian-American speaker, author, and holistic medicine counselor,

> In that light, the greatest gift of grace is that having created our own tragic circumstances, we are simultaneously capable of liberating ourselves. This, in essence, is the whole reason for the Law of Karma to exist—as a means of insuring that there is enough equipoise between light and darkness that no one is ever truly lost, damned, or devoid of a path to enlightenment. ("Is Karma Fair?" 2014)

How might a Christian respond to the above view of human "liberation"? How should a Christian respond to the existentialist's view that we are alone in the universe and must save ourselves? Worldview thinking is the process of identifying the worldview perspectives in what we read, hear, and see, and then comparing and contrasting them with the answers provided by our own worldview. This mindset is the first step toward worldview integration.

Let's look at a few pantheistic quotes as we did for naturalism last chapter. Try to critique these thoughts in light of your Christian worldview.

"I Am Eternal Spirit"

Chopra, who was no doubt influenced by the Hinduism of his country of birth and, by his own admission, other mystical leaders of the East, said the following:

> I know myself as the immeasurable potential of all that was, is, and will be.... There is no other I than the entire universe. I am being and I am nowhere and everywhere at the same time. I am omnipresent, omniscient; I am eternal spirit that animates everything in existence. (1992)

Take particular note of his claim to be all that "was, is, and will be." Carl Sagan used similar language about the cosmos; the Berenstain Bears said the same about nature. But who is correct? Is the human self all that *was, is, and ever will be*, or is it the cosmos? These worldviews are mutually exclusive, and both are contrary to a Christian worldview.

"My Own Power"

Many popular books written in the 1980s and '90s revealed the influence of Westernized pantheism. Gloria Steinem's book *Revolution from Within*, for example, championed several controversial ideas previously foreign to the Western mind, such as the pagan prayer/poem by Robin Morgan, "Network of the Imaginary Mother."

> Blessed be my brain
>
> that I may conceive of *my own power.*
>
> Blessed be my breast
>
> that I may give sustenance to those I love.
>
> Blessed be my womb
>
> that I may create what I choose to create.
>
> Blessed be my knees

that I my bend so as not to break.

Blessed be my feet

that I may walk in the path of my highest will.

Steinem also quotes Eastern thinkers when she addresses human nature and self-esteem.

i found god in myself and i loved her,

i loved her fiercely.

—Ntozake Shange

The Lord of all,

The knower of all,

The *beginning and end of all*—

That *Self* dwells in every human heart."

—Upanishads

Several phrases above are italicized for emphasis. Note the use of the "beginning and end" terminology. Steinem called for meditation, trust, and confidence, but not in God. In fact, she said, "By the year 2000 we will, I hope, raise our children to believe in human potential, not God" (in the *Saturday Review of Education*, March 1973).

In the epilogue of *Dancing in the Light*, actress Shirley MacLaine, another self-proclaimed "New Ager," expresses many Eastern beliefs (reincarnation, past lives, spiritual guides, and the like). Some of her thoughts reflect a mix of existentialism and Eastern thought. She says that when she began to see the world through karmic consciousness and the knowledge that we all create our own paths, she began to think about life differently. She concluded her book this way:

"I know that I exist, therefore I AM. I know the God-source exists, therefore IT IS; Since I am part of that force, then I AM that I AM" (1985).

In light of Exodus 3:14, this is an audacious claim indeed.

Alternatives to Naturalistic Determinism

According to Westernized pantheism—otherwise known as New Age thinking—you are God, I am God, and the trees are God. Everything is God, and God is everything. Man, according to one of India's contemporary philosophers, "is God in the temporary state of self-forgetfulness" (Zacharias 2000).

New Ageism features elements of Gnosticism, Hinduism, Buddhism, spiritualism /animism, mysticism, and Taoism. What a conglomeration; anything goes! The movement promotes a number of practices, including palm reading, séances, channeling, guru guides, meditation, reincarnation, exploration of past lives, occultism, paganism, and worship of Gaia/Mother Earth.

The Impact of Eastern Thought on Education

Eastern/New Age thinking endorsed turning inward and trusting ourselves to find meaning, and this perspective has seeped into the language of teachers: "You can be anything you want to be if you want it badly enough!" "Just believe in yourself!" After all, you are god.

A second cultural mantra is "You must love yourself first; turn inward before turning outward." Allan Bloom referred to this as one of the myths that high school students carry with them into their university years that leads to self-centeredness. He writes, "The psychology of the self has succeeded so well that it is now the instinct of most of us to turn for a cure for our ills back within ourselves" (1987).

In *The Closing of the American Mind*, Bloom not only spoke to the issue of turning inward, but also to the practice of believing everything—and, consequently, believing *nothing*. He warned that the result would be the death of critical thinking and would lead to close-mindedness. Believing that all ideas are equally valid is irrational.

> Openness used to be the virtue that permitted us to seek the good by using reason. It now means accepting everything and denying reason's power.... Prejudices ... are visions about the way things are.... The mind that has no prejudices at the outset is empty.

To think critically, one must believe in something in particular, even if the belief is only partially true (or entirely wrong). This is true when developing a biblical worldview as well. The pantheistic belief that all paths lead to the same place is an irrational one; it leads to a society that has abandoned reason and educational enterprises that cannot develop critical thinkers.

These mantras began as an attempt to salvage the value and worth of human beings in some way that had been lost under dehumanizing naturalistic worldviews. The newer views placed the focus on the self and turning within. Strangely enough, however, pantheism also dehumanizes the person, because it views individual personhood as an illusion. Pantheists who hold to life after death believe that the ultimate goal is to become one with the impersonal "All," at which time individuality ceases to be.

The Subtle Self-Focus in School Curriculum

When I was just beginning to develop a worldview approach to biblical integration, I substituted for a second grade teacher in the school where I was interim principal. One of the stories in the second grade reader was about a Native American boy who had been born sickly. In the story, his grandfather tells him that his name means strength, and that if the boy repeats his name over and over, all will be well. Spurred by my newfound fascination with integration, I quickly wrote several activities to accompany the book. Students were to read to find out the answers to the questions. The two below were in the teacher's edition.

- In our story today, the little boy has a big problem in life. What is it?
- His grandfather tries to help him with the problem. What does his grandfather tell him to do?

The following questions led into worldview integration:

- To whom might you talk when you have a problem?
- If you had been the friend of this boy, what might you have told him to help him with his problem? Why?
- What else could you have done to help him?
- If we know of someone who has this kind of problem, what might we do?

Several worldview questions are addressed and answered in this story.

What is a human being? One who talks. To whom can we talk when we are in need? To *ourselves*—implying that we have the ability to fix ourselves. However, the Christian worldview also posits that there is someone else we can talk to: God, the creator of the universe.

1. *What is a human being?* As image-bearers of God, we are communicators by nature. We talk because God talks. This is a *connection* to the story.

2. *Is there someone powerful enough to help solve our problems—is there a God?* There is a God; He listens when we talk to Him, loves and cares, and can help us; He designed our family and uses others to help. This *connects* the story to a Christian worldview in that we can depend on loved ones who care for us such as parents and caretakers; it also *distinguishes* that there is one higher than we or our parents or ourselves, the living God, with whom we can talk. "The Lord is near to all who call on Him, to all who call on Him in truth" (Psalm 145:18).

3. How do we know right and wrong? It is right to show compassion to someone in need? It is right to "love your neighbor" and show compassion like the grandpa did. Jesus tells us it is right and when we do this we are more like Him. This *connects* to the story's positive portrayal of the grandfather's kindness. "Be kind and compassionate to one another" (Ephesians 4:32a). It also reinforces the truth that we get our "beliefs" from God's Word.

The story focused on the power of *language*—the last sentence of the story was "Isn't it wonderful that we have the gift of language to talk to ourselves in times of need?" I led the class in a discussion of the value of language and asked why God would choose to communicate to humans using the Bible. Answer: because He made us to be communicators by nature. We talk because He talks. Even second graders can connect with this concept if it is familiar.

I asked the class what they thought about the last sentence in the story and whether or not they might have a better idea. One little boy replied, "When I get hurt, I don't talk to myself. I talk to my mommy." Another child said, "We can talk to God, too." This led to a good discussion on communicating with God and parents, connecting the story to a Christian worldview.

Finally, the students made encouragement cards for a classmate who had been sick and out of school for several days. Students wrote on the cards, "We are talking to God and asking Him to make you better. He cares for you." This not only encouraged the sick classmate; it served as a connective activity. Compassion and love are Christlike qualities. The activity connects the story to axiology—the philosophical study of values—and answers "How do we know right and wrong?"

ACTIVITY

Read through the curriculum materials for your grade level and be alert for pantheistic views; use the chart provided in this chapter to identify them. Is the universe seen as a living organism encompassing all that exists? Do you find references to the earth and humans being all of one basic "stuff"? Are there references to meditation, listening to the world, or listening to one's own heart? This is a distinction process.

Next, try to identify topics and subject areas that clearly correlate with the foundational belief that God exists (even if the God of the Bible is not mentioned). Is intelligent design seen in the creation? Is the earth to be cared for and use but not abused? Cite places where humans, created in the image of God, are inventive, creative, communicative, expressive, etc. Plan to connect these to a biblical worldview.

Eight

Naturalistic Pantheism

Pantheism and naturalism have made something of a truce in the West. With the discovery of quantum field theory and the newer theories of time and space, the scientific world has become far more comfortable tweaking the naturalistic worldview. The unsatisfying answers to major worldview questions have also promoted a broad new form of "spirituality." There is growing interest in a worldview that can address both the natural external world and the inner world of humankind.

Rebecca Newberger Goldstein calls for the field of philosophy to arbitrate the divide between science and the humanities, even if the arbitration is not always appreciated.

She writes in the Chronicle Review,

> We lead conceptually compartmentalized lives, our points of view balkanized so that we can live happily with our internal tensions and contradictions, many of the borders fortified by *unexamined presumptions*. It's the job of philosophy to undermine that happiness, and it's been at it ever since the Athenians showed their gratitude to Socrates for services rendered by offering him a cupful of hemlock. (2014; emphasis added)

Philosophy as a discipline takes pride in the examination of underlying assumptions. But often this is done in language only the philosopher can comprehend. Scientists, who have not studied philosophy, may not be able to identify their own assumptions and thus move forward with an arrogant self-assurance that their view is free of bias—"just the facts." When challenged by philosophers, the scientists simply dismiss the challenge by placing philosophy into a category other than truth; only science can yield "true knowledge." The naturalistic worldview once crowded the humanities out of high academia, but times are changing.

The movement to avoid compartmentalization may have contributed to a popular attempt to bring together the sciences and the humanities, spawning the development of a worldview that combines naturalism and pantheism. This syncretism is shaping the thought-world of many Americans in the general culture and penetrating school curriculum. It is called naturalistic pantheism.

The man on the street is reading literature and Internet posts that promote this emerging worldview conglomerate. Take for example this post by Deepak Chopra:

> It's commonly accepted that science and spirituality are not compatible. Science is considered our reliable way forward, while spirituality is often regarded as a sentimental relic of our past we can't quite let go of. So to say it is necessary for the two to work together may seem unrealistic. For centuries, science has led our progress; spirituality, as indicated through participation in orthodox religion, has been in steady decline. But the *unorganized, personal aspect of spirituality is the subjective pursuit of value, reality, and understanding through individual experience or consciousness.* This aspect of spirituality has not declined. ("Our Future Depends on Spirituality and Science Working Together"; emphasis added)

The beliefs of this new hybrid will *not* be found in the books or websites of prominent atheistic naturalists. Instead, you will find it described on websites that have espoused both spirituality and naturalism and are now revising their worldview to fit with the modern longing for meaning. The worldview addressed here has been labeled naturalistic pantheism, world pantheism, religious naturalism, or scientific pantheism; however, it is much closer to naturalism than to pantheism.

Richard Dawkins described pantheism as "sexed-up atheism" in *The God Delusion*. He defends his claim by saying that pantheists do not believe in a supernatural god at all, but use the word as a non-supernatural synonym for nature, or the universe, or for the lawfulness that governs its workings (2006). His label is verified on the official website of world pantheism:

> So what's the difference between atheism and pantheism? As far as disbelief in supernatural beings, forces, or realms, there is no difference.... However, pantheism goes further, and adds to atheism an embracing, positive, and reverential feeling about our lives on planet Earth, our place in Nature and the wider universe.... It's a form of spirituality that is totally compatible with science. (http://www.pantheism.net/atheism.htm)

In some ways, despite the major differences among them, naturalism, pantheism, and naturalistic pantheism are *one major naturalistic* view of the world.

The Naturalistic Pantheism Worldview

The statements below are taken from the official website of naturalistic pantheism (http://www.pantheism.net/manifest.htm) and represent the current thinking of this worldview. Certain phrases have been italicized for emphasis.

Reality is a "*single kind of substance*, energy/matter, which is vibrant and infinitely creative in all its forms." Naturalistic pantheism is a monistic worldview, just like traditional naturalism and Eastern pantheism. Everything that exists is of one essence. The nineteenth and early twentieth century naturalists held that everything is made up of matter; mid-twentieth and twenty-first century naturalists hold that everything is made of matter and energy, opening the door to the recognition of the "energy force" of the universe described by many Eastern pantheists.

"We *revere and celebrate* the universe as the totality of being, past, present and future. It is self-organizing, ever-evolving, and inexhaustibly diverse. Its overwhelming power, beauty, and fundamental mystery compel the *deepest human reverence and wonder.*"

Theirs is a call to worship nature and the universe. The universe is "what was, is, and is to come," just as it is for the traditional naturalist. The twist is that nature and, by extension, humankind should be worshipped. "We take the real universe and nature as our starting and finishing point, not some preconceived idea of God."

To judge truth, "we honor reality, and keep our minds open to *the evidence of the senses and of science's* unending quest for deeper understanding. These are our best *means of coming to know the universe*, and on them we base our aesthetic and religious feelings about reality."

Notice that science is still the way to deeper understanding; however, values and religious *feelings* are acknowledged as part of the human condition. This is a departure from the naturalistic view, which does not consider values and religion to have any real truth value.

What about humans? "We are an integral part of nature, which we should cherish, revere, and preserve in all its magnificent beauty and diversity. We should strive to live in harmony with nature locally and globally." Humans have value as part of nature. This view is directed toward reestablishing some worth and purpose for humanity in spite of the logical conclusions of naturalism.

The Major Differences

There are some major differences between Eastern pantheism and naturalistic pantheism. In the naturalistic version, every individual has direct access—through perception, emotion and meditation—to ultimate reality. There is no need for the mediation by priests, gurus, or revealed Scriptures utilized in Eastern pantheism (and its Westernized cousin, New Ageism).

What happens when a person dies? All three of these nontheistic worldviews hold that individuality ceases to exist at death. Naturalistic pantheists, like naturalists, see death as the return of our *elements* to nature and the end of our existence. In both naturalistic pantheism and naturalism, the forms of "afterlife" available to humans are *natural* ones. Naturalistic pantheism, however, emphasizes that our actions, ideas, and memories live on. Our genes live on in our families, and our elements are endlessly recycled in nature (a form of reincarnation of decomposed matter). This is an attempt to soften the cold naturalistic view of death.

In the Eastern version of pantheism, especially Hinduism, the soul exists and lives on; it is reincarnated to again experience life until it finally receives ultimate enlightenment and gets off the cosmic treadmill. The ultimate goal is to become one with the One, losing the illusion of individuality and the experience of duality. (There are variations on the concept of death among Eastern worldviews.)

There are elements of naturalism and Eastern pantheism in naturalistic pantheism, and some of these underlying assumptions are taking education by storm. There is also some crossover between naturalistic pantheism and philosophical Taoism.

Naturalistic Pantheism

Metaphysics: Issues of Existence	Ultimate reality is the Universe. Humans are part of that energy/matter. After death, we return to nature; our elements, memories, and offspring continue. No reincarnation of individual persons.
Epistemology: Issues of Knowing	Humans know truth through science and the study of nature. The method for truth-judging is conscious awareness of nature: perception, emotion, meditation.
Axiology: Issues of Valuing	Humans are "equal centers of awareness" of the universe, and thus deserve reverence and respect. Moral values are decided by individuals or groups. There is no basis for judging right and wrong.

Naturalistic pantheism has been shaped by Buddhism, Hinduism, and Taoism, but it contains much more naturalism than pantheism. Physicist Frijof Capra, heavily influenced by Eastern mysticism, wrote:

> The basic recurring theme in Hindu mythology is the creation of the world by the self-sacrifice of God—"sacrifice" in the original sense of "making sacred"—whereby God becomes the world which, in the end, becomes again God. This creative activity of the Divine is called lila, the play of God, and the world is seen as the stage of the divine play.... In the Hindu view of nature ... the dynamic force of the play is karma.... It is the active principle of the play, the total universe in action, where everything is dynamically connected with everything else. In the words of the Gita, Karma is the force of creation, wherefrom all things have their life. (1975)

The naturalistic pantheist would avoid using the term God unless it is clearly viewed as nature. They might say that the divine stage is the universe. There is no mystical creative higher power such as Brahman as held in Hinduism. Terms like *maya* and *karma* seem to be avoided in the naturalistic version as well. But there is a huge focus on caring for the universe and Mother Nature. It is this reverence for nature that comes through curriculum materials today.

In 2008, nuclear physicist Amit Goswami wrote *God Is Not Dead,* a presentation of a new paradigm for science in which he argues for the "god hypothesis" based upon quantum physics (the book shares no relation to the 2013 film of the same name). Goswami's god, however, is not the God of the Bible—or, indeed, of any popular religion. He writes,

> The popular version of Christianity tells us that both the material universe and God are real. The new science tells us that the universe, God, and we are not really separate.... In the view of quantum physics, all attempts to distinguish between nature and "supernature" have lost complete credibility.... Here God and spirituality are recovered in the sense of an immanent God, or a "Gaia consciousness" immanent throughout the whole world with all its organisms.

At the end of his book, he advocates for a switch from a "matter-based" worldview to one based on quantum physics. But this worldview is still unapologetically monistic.

The current move to integrate naturalism and pantheism in the West reflects the recognition that humans are something more than biological machines. A worldview that does not address this "something more" cannot be coherent or ultimately satisfying. Naturalistic pantheism attempts to welcome both those who worship at the altar of science and those who view the natural world as an extension of the universal "One." The merged view has concluded that humans need to be affirmed, even adored, as part of the material reality. This results in self-worship; the *self* has taken center stage in life as the measure of truth and moral principles. This may be the underlying worldview of the narcissistic "Selfie" generation.

Societal Benefits of "Spirituality"

The study of religion by some atheistic naturalists has offered answers as to why "spirituality" is important to humans. Some have concluded that there is evolutionary benefit to the revering of capital-N Nature and the things that sustain human life. The sun, water, plants, animals, and so on have been held in ultimate esteem by those who do not know God.

This sort of "spirituality" is shared by the philosophers of Mars Hill, whom the Apostle Paul said were "in every way ... very religious" (Acts 17:22). But they did not know the God of creation. Paul spoke to them about the "unknown god," whom they worshiped in case they had missed one. Paul's contribution to their thinking was to share the God of the Bible, who "gives everyone life and breath and everything else" (17:25). God did this so that they "would seek Him and perhaps reach out for Him" (17:27a). Humans have a propensity to worship what they find important in sustaining their lives. It is not unusual to find worldviews that ultimately worship the creation rather than the Creator.

A Christian View of Nature

The Christian views nature in light of the stewardship commanded by God. We are to care for and use—but not abuse—the resources God has created. But we are to worship the Creator rather than the creation, and this distinction is crucial for truly biblical thinking. Romans 1:25a makes it clear that humans can turn God's pattern for things upside-down: "They exchanged the truth about God for a lie, and worshiped and served created things rather than the Creator." This is true of all three worldviews addressed in these chapters; they end up worshipping what God has made.

Sample Curriculum Materials to Analyze

Susan Jeffers' book *Brother Eagle, Sister Sky*, a resource often suggested for social studies units on Native Americans or as a supplementary material for Earth Day, contains strong hints of naturalistic pantheism. As you read the excerpt below, identify concepts that *connect* to a biblical view of the land and *distinguish* those that do not.

> My father said to me,
> I know the sap that courses through the trees

as I know the blood that flows in my veins.
We are part of the earth and it is part of us.
The perfumed flowers are our sisters.
The bear, the deer, the great eagle, these are our brothers.
The rocky crests, the meadows, the ponies—all belong to the same family.

The voice of my ancestors said to me,
The shining water that moves in the streams and rivers is
not simply water, but the blood of your grandfather's grandfather....
The water's murmur is the voice of your great-great-grandmother.
The rivers are our brothers....
You must give to the rivers the kindness you would give to any brother.
The voice of my grandfather said to me,
The air is precious. It shares its spirit with all the life it supports.
The wind that gave me my first breath also received my last sigh.
You must keep the land and air apart and sacred,
as a place where one can go to taste the wind that
is sweetened by the meadow flowers....

My ancestors said to me, This we know:
The earth does not belong to us.
We belong to the earth....

This we know:
All things are connected like the blood that unites us.
We did not weave the web of life,
We are merely a strand in it.
Whatever we do to the web, we do to ourselves.

The worldview thinking of the teacher is the first necessary element in using a worldview approach to biblical integration. You do not need to know about every tenet of every worldview to do this, but you do need to know what you *believe.*

For example, the careful and effective care for the earth and its creatures is one of the God-given duties of human beings. Christians should not only know their role in caring for the environment, but execute it to the best of their ability. However, God is not the earth and the earth is not God. Our Creator made the earth to be inhabited and gave humans a mandate to care for it. The earth is the Lord's, and we belong to Him—not to the earth. "The earth is the Lord's, and everything in it, the world, and all who live in it" (Psalm 24:1).

Is it the *wind* that provides my first breath and receives my last breath? No! God Himself gives all men life and breath and everything else! (Acts 17:25).

Would I use this book in spite of its worldview? Absolutely! Not only does it provide background information for understanding Native American culture and history, it addresses some things that Christians should be addressing in the care of the earth. It offers an opportunity to contrast a biblical view with a pantheistic view. It may also provide context about missionaries like David Brainerd, who needed to understand the Native Americans' reverence for nature in order to teach them about God.

"The Earth Is My Mother," a catchy song by Carol Johnson, is another example of reverence for the earth rather than the Creator of the earth. It is suggested for use with Earth Day activities in the social studies curriculum.

Here are some of the words:

> The earth is my mother
> She's good to me
> She gives me everything that I ever need
>
> Food on the table
> The clothes I wear
> The sun and the water.....
>
> The earth is my mother and my best friend, too
> The great provider for me and you
> Her ways are gentle, her life is strong . . .
> The earth is my mother and my best friend, too
> The great provider for me and you

How would you integrate this song with a biblical worldview? Gratitude for food and clothes is a wonderful idea; however, the songwriter refers to the earth as a living organism, a mother. Remember the words of the naturalistic pantheism manifesto? "We revere and celebrate the universe.... It is self-organizing, ever-evolving, and inexhaustibly diverse. Its overwhelming power, beauty and fundamental mystery compel the deepest human reverence and wonder."

This echoes the "humanist prayer" written by Lester Mondale, which first appeared in the spring 1983 edition of *Free Inquiry*.

> The world of stars, atoms, hills, trees, the source and final repository of my being, has become increasingly my beloved home—worthy of the ultimate in environmental devotion. I need no reinforcing and guiding revelation of divine command.

In other words, "I lift up my eyes to the hills, my beginning point and final repository; blessed be the hills!" This is not much different than assigning the starting point and final point to the wind or earth, but entirely different from the Christian view espoused in Psalm 121:1–2.

As Christians using materials written and edited by those whose worldviews differ from ours, how should we approach the strategic design of curriculum? Avoiding all non-Christian materials is impossible and may not be the best when teaching for worldview integration. True biblical worldview integration should include many opportunities for children to differentiate worldviews and strengthen a growing and informed *Christian* worldview.

The Danger of "Spiritual" Naturalism

In a recent interview, Nick Sagan, son of *Cosmos* host and popular scientist Carl Sagan, addressed why many atheists, agnostics, and secular humanists appreciated his father:

> I've met secular humanists who grew up in evangelical households, for whom *Cosmos* was their *first exposure to a scientific way of viewing the world*. Dad was a difference-maker. He reached out to people. He took them by the awe and wonder we feel over the most important questions we can think to imagine. He pulled them away from *blind faith*, away from pseudoscience, toward a deeper, richer understanding of the universe. (2014; emphasis added)

Sagan's son reminisced about one of his father's favorite sayings: "Science is not only compatible with spirituality; it is a profound source of spirituality." He went on to tell the interviewer, "You don't have to be religious to feel awe. All you have to do is look up at the stars." To him, spirituality is the sense of reverence inspired by the universe.

The language of "spirituality" and "faith" used in describing naturalism can be confusing to many in our culture today, especially our youth. Naturalism and pantheism have been synthesized to offer a new, attractive alternative to theism, one that merges cold naturalistic thinking with the extreme mysticism of pantheistic thought.

Our youth are exposed to the questions about ultimate reality and given false answers. Popular websites have promoted the integration of science and spirituality ever since Chopra's televised visit with Oprah Winfrey. One post on the Huffington Religion blog proposes an approach that integrates science and spirituality (but is devoid of a belief in the transcendent, personal God of the Bible) as the answer to the problems of humankind. But this focus on spirituality is deceptive. Chopra writes:

The scale of our planet's problems is too great to be solved without an integrated approach of science and spirituality. The power of consciousness needs the systemization of the scientific method, and the tools of science depend on the wisdom and creativity of individual consciousness to guide it in a meaningful direction. ("Our Future Depends on Spirituality and Science Working Together," 2014)

Are science and religion converging? No, according to Richard Dawkins. There are modern scientists whose words sound religious but whose beliefs, on closer examination, turn out to be identical to those of scientists who would call themselves atheists or atheistic naturalists.

Conclusion

After looking briefly at the three worldviews described in the last three chapters, a teacher might ask how these alternative worldviews have impacted their academic culture. More specifically, what has been the impact on Christian academic institutions?

Naturalism has led to duplicity, the dividing of worldviews into secular and sacred, academic and personal, public and private. School is seen as secular; church, chapel, or devotions are sacred. This leads to a disintegrated mind unable to love the Lord wholeheartedly.

Pantheism leads to a mystical, spiritual view of life and dismisses the value of academics. It may lead to a life of seeking a higher consciousness rather than God's truth. God's sovereignty in all things, including all domains of knowledge, is undermined by pantheistic thought.

Naturalistic pantheism is even more dangerous to the Christian mind in that it disguises atheistic naturalism with the language of spirituality. It promotes care for the environment (a biblical idea) and care for humans (also a biblical idea), but ultimately leads to worship of created things instead of the Creator.

Christian philosopher Francis Schaeffer spoke to the implications of the worldviews addressed in these last three chapters. He wrote in *A Christian Manifesto* (1981) that Christians have very gradually become disturbed over permissiveness, pornography, the public schools, the breakdown of the family, and finally abortion. He concluded:

> But they have not seen this as a totality—each thing being a part, a symptom, of a much larger problem. They have failed to see that all of this has come about due to a shift in world view—that is, through a fundamental change in the overall way people think and view the world and life as a whole. This shift has been *away from* a world

view that was at least vaguely Christian in people's memory (even if they were not individually Christian) *toward* something completely different—toward a world view based upon the idea that the final reality is impersonal matter or energy shaped into its present form by impersonal chance.

Cultural mores have worsened since Schaeffer's prescient manifesto. Nontheistic thought-forms and ideas have penetrated the culture, media, and school curricula. Teachers at Christian institutions must be aware of these and other popular non-Christian ideas if they are to train young minds for a complex and often confrontational culture.

ACTIVITY

1. In what ways are the beliefs of naturalistic pantheism more like naturalism than pantheism?

2. Using the chart in this chapter, identify examples of naturalistic pantheism in your curriculum.

3. In what major ways does a biblical worldview differ from the three worldviews addressed in the last three chapters?

4. Critique the following quote, taken from pantheism.net. What connects with a Christian worldview and what does not?

> SCIENTIFIC PANTHEISM reveres the universe and nature. It fuses religion and science, and concern for humans with concern for nature. It provides the most realistic concept of life after death, and the most solid basis for environmental ethics. It is a religion that requires no faith other than common sense, no revelation other than open eyes and a mind open to evidence, no guru other than your own self.

Nine

Christian Theism: The Integrating Core

Asking and answering the big questions of life is rarely easy. Usually, a worldview question is only examined after a major life event—often a catastrophe.

For many years, even before I became a Christian, I believed that after death, people either went to be with God or were separated from Him forever. After I became a Christian, I developed a better understanding of what awaits after life on earth. I learned that the body would decay in the grave or be cremated, but be resurrected one day. I learned that on the day of resurrection a new body would be reunited with the immaterial part of me that is present with the Lord and that the new body would be incorruptible. I learned that God wants humans, even after life, to have bodies and be whole as humans—not as angels or spirits only. I learned that "to be absent from the body is to be present with the Lord."

The real appreciation for this "big idea" knowledge did not hit me until my husband died, hardly a year after my father had passed away. It was then that the worldview question, "What happens when a person dies?" became more than a belief to be discussed in small group or a theology course. It was part of my human story.

I was in the ER room with my arm around my husband's shoulders when the doctor pronounced his death. My first *reaction* was to say, through tears, "Now you are with the Lord, your Savior, whom you love."

Both the nurse and the doctor cried with me. The nurse wondered out loud how I could bear to say what I had. But I never planned to say anything; the words just rolled off of my tongue. It was what I really believed to be true.

My deepening appreciation for this "big idea" was most noticeable to me in my prayer life in the days following Don's death. I remember telling the Lord I had no clue what it was really like to be "absent from the body but present with the Lord," or whether those who were in the Lord's presence cared about what went on here below. I asked the Lord to tell Don that I love him and miss him. I still do this sometimes. I have no way of knowing whether this is appropriate to ask of God, but I do know that the request represents a truth I hold deeply: that Don is indeed in His presence. The details are still fuzzy, but ever since, Easter has been a more glorious celebration for me. The resurrection of Christ, and of Christians, is more than a belief to be stated. It was embedded in my experience.

I mention this story for three reasons: first, to illustrate the importance of answers to worldview questions in real life; second, to demonstrate that worldview answers are broad and basic, and only become nuanced as we experience more of life; and last, to illustrate that our worldview answers may remain incomplete until we are in the Lord's presence one day. Worldview thinking and worldview integration are not just academic activities. The process of integration is never complete on this side of heaven.

Of course, I experienced this worldview-refining loss when I was already a mature adult. How would it work with elementary, secondary, or college students?

A Telephone Call

"Mrs. MacCullough," the girl on the phone said, "I need you to tell my mother what my sister did in your class."

The girl was a friend of my daughter. Early in my career, I taught at a Christian middle school; the girl's older sister had been a student in my seventh grade class.

"My sister was in a car accident two days ago," the girl continued. "And Mom is…."

She handed her mother the phone.

The mother's grief and trauma were readily apparent even before she spoke. I told her who I was, and how very sorry I was to hear about her loss. Then I told her how her daughter had come to me after Bible class to ask me how she could become a true Christian. I assured the woman that, based upon the Word of God, her child was in God's presence right now.

I don't know if my words comforted the mother, but I am certain they were a comfort for the younger sister, who had just started high school. The sister had come to know the Lord in third grade; she knew the biblical answer to what happens when a person dies. That belief comforted her during this time of grief and pain. She desperately wanted her mom to know that answer as well. This is worldview thinking and living!

The last three chapters have provided broad examples of the cultural worldviews vying for the hearts and minds of our students. In this chapter, we will finally look at the worldview which, in my opinion, offers the best and most complete answers to life's biggest questions.

A Biblical Worldview

The Christian worldview is a theistic worldview: its foundation is neither matter nor some impersonal universal force. Rather, Christian theism is a worldview that starts with the existence of a transcendent and personal God who created all that is and desires relationship with humankind. God is separate from His creation in His being. The cosmos did not flow out of His essence. He is God and we are not. He is our Creator, and we are His creation.

The other major theistic worldviews are Judaism and Islam. However, these two significantly differ from biblical Christianity, particularly in their beliefs about the nature of God. The Christian worldview informed by God's revealed word, holds that there is only one God who exists eternally in three persons. He is relational by nature, and Christ is, in His very nature, God.

Judaism and Islam do not accept the claim that Jesus Christ is God. Christian theism embraces both Old and New Testament, and is a framework of basic beliefs informed by the Bible. It is a qualitatively different alternative to all other worldviews including other theistic views. (Although it contains "theism" in its name, pantheism is not a theistic worldview.)

Christian Theism as a Worldview

Christian Contours, edited by Douglas Huffman, is a resource book I have used in my college courses. What I like most about the book is the set of questions it poses about a Christian worldview: Is there just one biblical worldview? What is the relationship of worldviews to truth? What is the biblical worldview? How do we handle disagreements between Christians regarding worldviews? It is important to answer some of these questions before developing a worldview approach to biblical integration.

Just One Biblical Worldview?

Whether there is only one biblical worldview is a particularly important question to missionaries and teachers working in national and international schools around the globe. There are differences of opinion on the issue; much of the difference occurs because of the way a worldview is described. Some Christians suggest there is an African-Christian worldview, an Asian-Christian worldview, a North American-Christian worldview, a European-Christian worldview, and so on. There is tremendous validity in addressing how cultural thinking is embedded in one's worldview. However, one of the biggest problems related to effective biblical worldview integration that I see is the thinking that cultural differences make biblical integration impossible. This flawed thinking has led to near-total abandonment of biblical integration. This is true of some Christian schools in the States as well, whose administrators and teachers cite the problems that arise when there are six or more denominations represented in their schools.

With the above in mind, this book treats the Christian worldview as biblical answers to the big questions of life. These might be considered the basic orthodoxy of Christianity. When speaking of Christians, then, I am not here referring to *cultural* Christians (who think they are Christians because they were born in a Christian country and believe in a higher power) but to Christians who understand the primacy of the Bible in the development of a Christian worldview.

Theologian J.P. Moreland writes that a worldview is more than just a set of beliefs. It includes the *rational structure* that occurs among the set of beliefs.

> A person's worldview contains two important features. First, it includes the *set of beliefs* the person accepts, especially those about important matters such as reality, God, value, knowledge, and so on....
>
> In general, the more central a belief is, the greater would be the change in one's worldview if the belief were abandoned. Central beliefs support and give justification to more peripheral ones. Belief in the reality of God, the faithfulness and reliability of the Bible, and the deity and humanity of Christ are central to a Christian worldview. (2007; emphasis added)

It is the basic or central beliefs that we will refer to in this chapter rather than those that, while important, are peripheral to core worldview issues (such as modes of baptism, communion, church polity, and what sort of music is appropriate in church). The task of a worldview approach to biblical integration is to bring one's developing life view, with all of its cultural baggage, into conformity with the perspective found in the Bible.

Informed and Conformed

James Sire described a worldview as "a fundamental orientation of the heart that can be expressed as a story or a set of presuppositions" that express our view of reality. Developing a *Christian (biblical)* worldview may be thought of as the adjusting of one's personal story to God's story. The standard for worldview integration then, is God's perspective as given in Scripture, rather than any particular cultural view of peripheral issues. God's Word is the standard for all Christians everywhere: North America, South America, Western and Eastern Europe, Asia, and in fact, any continent of the globe.

The Christian Worldview as a Unique Story

The rational structure for the Christian worldview begins and ends with the existence of a personal, sovereign God. This is where the Apostle Paul began when he contrasted biblical Christianity to the worldview of the Greek philosophers on Mars Hill. "The God who made the world and everything in it is the Lord of heaven and earth and does not live in temples built by human hands. And he is not served by human hands, as if he needed anything. Rather, he himself gives everyone life and breath and everything else" (Acts 17:24–25). The history of the universe and humankind is His story.

The concept of adjusting one's worldview to the biblical story coincides with research suggesting the power of story. Humans have a propensity for learning through a narrative format. Current day use of "story" in history and other academic classes is yielding good results for learning as well. It is a good idea, in my opinion, to have students occasionally use the story format to describe the story of God's creation, humankind's fall, and Christ's redemptive sacrifice. The story will become more detailed as the students progress from elementary into high school, perhaps culminating in a senior project of writing the whole story. This type of activity complements the philosophy of life paper required of seniors in many Christian academic institutions.

The Christian Worldview as Answers to the Big Questions of Life

This book uses the question and answer approach, rather than the story format, for curricular integration (though the questions approach is complementary to the story format). When teaching in a Christian school setting, the regular curriculum will address various worldview questions, but very rarely in a way that fits with the story format. These questions must be addressed as a part of the regular curriculum. When big foundational questions are addressed and answered by comparing a Christian worldview answer to the implied or stated worldview question and answer in the materials, the process is specific to that *particular* lesson. The result may be that that the student does not, at the time, rehearse the whole story, but rather deals with a particular part of the story. These parts can eventually be organized into "His Story" as a culminating paper, theology paper, or philosophy paper.

Humans have a tendency to fit in new knowledge with old to make sense out of incoming information. The process of fitting in seems to be a human characteristic that functions in the learning process. We often ask questions when current information and beliefs conflict with new information. New information may cause cognitive dissonance or disequilibrium unless students have been conditioned to think that in school, teachers do the thinking and the students take notes. By our nature, we seek answers to dispel the disequilibrium that occurs when old knowledge conflicts with incoming information. Dispelling cognitive dissonance helps to create coherency and may also motivate students and teachers toward further study and research. Coherency is one of the goals of a well-thought out, internally consistent worldview. It is a necessary, but not sufficient, characteristic of a well-developed worldview. Humans can be consistent and coherent in their set of beliefs and still be wrong as measured by God's view of things.

Describing a Christian Worldview

Reality is often expressed in terms of the framework of existence, often using the terms what *was*, what *is*, and what *will be*. Carl Sagan opened *Cosmos* with the statement that the cosmos is all that has *existed, exists, or will exist*. Deepak Chopra declared that he, himself, is *all that existed, exists, or will exist*. The Christian worldview begins with a different starting point for ultimate reality: the living God who has always *existed, exists now, and will exist forever*.

These three foundational beliefs yield very different views of the world, humanity, knowing—indeed, of all of life. Starting points matter!

Naturalism	Pantheism	Christian Theism
"The cosmos is all that is, or ever was, or ever will be."	"I know myself as the immeasurable potential of all that *was, is, and will be.* I am omnipresent, omniscient; I am eternal spirit that animates everything in existence."	"Holy, holy, holy is the Lord God Almighty, who was, and is, and is to come" (Revelation 4:8b). "I am the Alpha and the Omega," says the *Lord God,* "who is, and who was, and who is to come, the *Almighty*" (Revelation 1:8). "I am the Alpha and the Omega, the First and the Last, the Beginning and the End" (Revelation 22:13). " ... From everlasting to everlasting you are God" (Psalm 90:2b).

Only one of these views can be accurately describing the way things really are. In *The Question of God*, Armand Nicholi asked of the very different worldviews of Freud and Lewis:

> Are these worldviews merely philosophical speculations with no right or wrong answer? No. One of them begins with the basic premise that God does not exist, the other with the premise that He does. They are, therefore, mutually exclusive—if one is right, the other must be wrong. (2002)

Christianity cannot harmonize with naturalism because of its most fundamental belief! Likewise, it cannot harmonize with pantheistic mysticism.

Reality, Truth, and Beliefs: Components of a Worldview

Reality is "all that exists in the physical and spiritual realms. It is objective, existing independently of the perception of our five senses ... while there is an aspect of reality that is not immediately available to our five senses, much of reality is knowable through our senses" (Nelson, in Hoffman). This description of reality is written from a Christian perspective. Notice that both the physical and spiritual realms are included. A naturalist would say that reality is that which can be verified in the physical realm only. A pantheist would say that reality is located in the spiritual realm only; all else is illusion. Naturalistic pantheists have tried to bridge the gap by addressing humanity and nature as deified matter.

Postmodernism: A New Way of Thinking about Truth

Up to this point, the worldviews addressed have held to mutually exclusive foundational beliefs about ultimate reality: impersonal nature, an impersonal energy force or spirit, or a personal God. Postmodernists, on the other hand, would say that humans create their own reality. While postmodern thought is not a full-blown philosophy of life, it is impacting cultural thinking about reality and truth. While reality has been traditionally defined as that which actually exists, and truth as that which corresponds to reality, the anti-philosophy of postmodernism has replaced these definitions with the mantra that "Whatever one believes to be real is his own reality and the only reality he can ever know. Whatever one believes is truth to them." Two people can hold entirely contradictory beliefs and both be considered correct. The law of non-contradiction has been buried. In this view of knowledge and knowing, humans are truth *makers* rather than truth seekers.

In this postmodern way of thinking, there is no need for beliefs to correspond logically or rationally to the way things are. There is certainly no need for a person to bring his views into relationship with any other set of beliefs. This is one of the reasons that postmodernism has been described as the death of logic and an attack on reason: it spurns any external standard for truth. Postmodernism and cultural pluralism (briefly addressed in chapter five) are barriers to the development of a Christian worldview, especially in today's popular youth culture. For many youth today, all truth is "my truth." Christian educators must be aware of the tenor of the day and be diligent in challenging this cultural view of knowing.

Worldview Beliefs Accepted as True

Holders of different worldviews *believe* their view is the correct one. Believing sincerely, however, that something is true does not make it true (except for the die-hard postmodernist). No matter which view of reality one adopts, in order for the "truth claim" to be true, it must *correspond to what is actually the case.* For instance: Is there a personal, relational, holy God? What evidence is there for your belief? What is your source of evidence? Since reality, truth, and beliefs come together in a worldview, it is important that these three concepts be addressed, even in a cursory way, if one is to be serious about biblical integration. Winfried Corduan put it this way:

> There is some kind of reality that is constituted independently of what we say about it. In other words, either my car is in the parking lot or not; either the geometry of right triangles follows the Pythagorean theorem or not; either God exists or He does not. This reality is a given. Our statements are true if they correspond to the reality in question; they are false if they do not correspond. (1993)

Christians freely and humbly admit dependence upon the living God for our epistemological foundation. In biblically formed Christian theism, one's truth claims—that there is a personal and transcendent God who created all that is and has chosen to reveal Himself to His Creation—are true, if and only if, there actually is a caring and personal God. But the same criteria are used for the foundational beliefs of every worldview.

Each worldview is based on foundational assumptions, which are always a matter of *faith*. The naturalist has *faith* that all is matter; the pantheist has *faith* that all is spiritual. The Christian has *faith* that the Bible is a reliable source of truth (a claim that has been addressed many times without failing). Christianity claims truth itself is grounded in the character of God and is therefore absolute, objective, and sourced in God Himself. Humans are created with the capacity to come to know what God has provided to know: Himself and His created order—that is, all of reality!

Implication

Why take the time to address these concepts in a book written for Christian teachers who will create worldview activities for biblical integration? Today's students are impacted by naturalism, pantheism, pluralism, and postmodernism, all of which obstruct the pursuit of biblical truth. A Christian worldview claims to be based upon universal truth that corresponds to reality as God Himself has revealed it. Christians, both teachers and students, come together in humility to seek God's truth so that we can love and serve Him with undivided hearts.

ACTIVITY

"The standard that measures two things is something different from either." —C.S. Lewis

1. How does this quote relate to the task of Christian educators working with students in the development of a biblical worldview?

2. "Worldviews beliefs may be true, partially true, or entirely false." How does this statement relate to the development of worldview integration?

Ten

Expressing the Christian Worldview

Alfred:	Don't you think Professor Smith is right? It is childish to believe in God. We're in college now.
Mark:	No, I didn't agree with the professor. It is not absurd to believe in God! It is very reasonable.
Alfred:	You do believe there is a God?
Mark:	How else do you explain such a precisely crafted universe? We breathe perfectly constituted air, have enough water and heat to live and grow plants that give us food to survive. The sun is at a distance just right for Earth not to fry or freeze. How do you explain that we have personality, language, and a history that we can record?
Alfred:	You had better stop thinking like that, Mark, if you are going to survive here academically.
Mark:	Can you give me one good reason to stop thinking about the existence of God?
Alfred:	To pass Prof Smith's course!
Mark:	I mean an intelligent reason. Something based upon what you observe in nature and in life or in what you believe.
Alfred:	Mark, you won't make it here. It's just like Prof Smith said—anyone who believes in God is emotionally and academically immature. Grow up!
Mark:	Well, Alfred, I hope we can still be friends. Let's talk about this later.

While this is a contrived conversation, Alfred's view is not far removed from what is occurring today at colleges and universities when Christian young people arrive for study.

One result of *not* knowing what you believe and *not* understanding the process of growing intellectually is the temptation to personally attack people who think differently. Ideas are not debated based upon information but rather upon "my view versus yours." This practice of demeaning people rather than challenging ideas is evident in our culture today. When Christians do not know what they believe and why, they do not challenge non-Christian ideas, as Mark tried to do in the conversation above, but simply sit back in silence or attack the person or character of the one whose beliefs do not fit with theirs.

Biblical worldview integration is designed to help teachers and students develop a biblical perspective that can be discussed openly in the classroom using the word of God as the standard while respecting others who hold to other views. This is a necessity for Christian service and loving our neighbor. Knowing what you believe and why allow you to critique other views, connecting with or distinguishing from a biblical worldview, while loving the people who hold to different beliefs.

Expressing a Christian Worldview

Try to fill out the chart below according to your Christian worldview. Refer back to previous charts and the eight worldview questions listed earlier, if needed.

Worldview Issues	Worldview Concepts
Metaphysics: Issues of Existence	
Epistemology: Issues of Knowing	
Axiology: Issues of Valuing	

Christians might communicate their biblical beliefs about these issues differently, but in general, there would be agreement on the basic tenets. Below is one way to express some of the major issues in Christian worldview thinking.

Worldview Issues	Worldview Concepts
Metaphysics: Issues of Existence	An infinite, transcendent, personal, eternal God exists. God exists as a Trinity of Father, Son, and Holy Spirit; He created all that exists, including a finite, material world. He designed, created, and sustains the cosmos. The universe as we know it had a beginning and will have an end. Reality is both material and spiritual. God created humans in His image and made us to be material and immaterial in essence. He gave us a mandate to care for this planet; we have a purpose for being here—to reflect His character, His glory, and to be what He intended us to be, doing the work He ordained. Humans and creation are in an abnormal, dysfunctional state and need redemption.
Epistemology: Issues of Knowing	Humans are created with the capacity to come to know and have been given something to know: God and His created order. There is objective truth worth pursuing, and the human mind (despite being limited) has access to it. We use God's revealed Word and His world to grow in our understanding of who He is, who we are, and the nature of His created order. God is ultimate reality, He is truth and reveals truth; He has equipped humankind with reason and the five senses to use in discovering and discerning truth about Himself, ourselves, and the world; because of the Fall, these means are flawed and imperfect; humans need revealed truth found in God's Word and the guidance of God's Spirit to help make sense of His perspective.
Axiology: Issues of Valuing	Moral values/ethics are measured by God's character and are therefore not a "moving target." The good and the beautiful are inherent in God Himself. Neither the individual nor the group is the standard. God's character can be known universally. Humankind has been given a conscience: a capacity for coming to know right and wrong, good and bad, better and best. It must be educated and exercised because of the fall. Humans hate, lie, conduct violence, and make war because of sin. Jesus Christ died for the sins of humanity to restore our relationship with Him. We cannot work our way back to God. He has done the work and invites our response.

Below are some briefly stated answers to the eight questions posed by various alternative worldviews (adapted from *The Universe Next Door*, 2009). You might try to select the ones that you think fit with a biblical view of things and then think through and write out your answers in a more comprehensive format. Try to identify the views of the worldviews addressed earlier (naturalism, pantheism, and naturalistic pantheism). Views are separated by semicolons. The ability to identify worldview answers to questions that fit with a biblical view and those that do not, is also a part of the first element in developing worldview integration.

1. What is prime reality—the ultimate or foundational reality?

☐ Nature

☐ God

☐ Impersonal energy force

☐ The self

2. What is the nature of external reality, that is, the world around us?

☐ Here by chance

☐ An illusion

☐ The universe is one mind

☐ Designed, created, and sustained

3. What is a human being?

☐ Sleeping god and part of the soul of the universe

☐ Material only: a biological machine

☐ Part of the mind of the universe

☐ Created by God—in His image, special among all of His creation, but fallen and in need of redemption

4. What happens to a person at death?

☐ Decomposed matter, period

☐ The spirit awaits rebirth and ultimate release from the cycle

☐ Absent from the body but present in an eternal destination (heaven for believers, separation from God for nonbelievers)

5. How do we know anything that we think we know?

☐ Capacity evolved and is physiological, chemistry, electrical, hormonal

☐ Reminiscence of ideas from eternity or prior life

☐ Created with the capacity to know

6. How do we know what is right and wrong?

☐ Whatever we decide as a society—group consensus that promotes human survival

☐ Whatever I choose personally

☐ Right and wrong are ultimately illusions; the appearance of good and bad is the principle of karma

☐ Through what God has revealed in His Word and in His character

7. What is the meaning of human history?

☐ There is no meaning

☐ History is a human construct subject to interpretation and revision

☐ History is His story and is moving toward the fulfillment of His plan

8. What life commitments are consistent with these beliefs?

☐ Eat, drink, and be merry, for tomorrow you die

☐ Becoming self-actualized and making myself

☐ Enlightenment (becoming one with the All) by following a guru or other enlightened person

☐ Flourishing as a human, growing to be all that God intended me to be

It is worthwhile to determine biblical answers to these questions by studying God's revealed view of things in His Word, and perhaps by discussing the questions with colleagues, pastors, and Bible study groups. Appendix Two features several sets of answers from Christian theologians.

God's Word Is Truth

God's Word is truth, but it is not exhaustive truth; not all answers to the questions humans pose are found in the Bible. I might look for God's direction as I choose a vacation destination, but I will not find the name of the Canadian Rockies in the Bible. However, answers to life's *biggest* questions are there. The answer to what happens when a person dies is found in the Bible, even though it does not reveal everything God has prepared for the believer and the unbeliever at death.

Moreover, there is some room for uncertainty in biblical interpretation. Humans are limited in knowing God's revealed view perfectly. This makes worldview thinking deeply humbling. Believers have multiple resources to grow in the understanding of the Bible (God has given us the revelation of Jesus, and He promised to send the Holy Spirit to guide us in all truth). But this does not preclude study. The Sadducees had Scripture, but they still missed the message of Jesus and the truth of the resurrection. We must *study* Scripture with the knowledge that we are not perfect in our understanding.

An Eye-Opening Journey

After His resurrection, Jesus joined two of His followers walking on the road to Emmaus, but the two did not recognize Him. As they spoke to the "stranger," they told Him of the events of the past days: the One they had hoped would redeem Israel was crucified, and now His body was missing from the tomb. They were correct in their account, but they had incomplete knowledge of what had *really* happened.

What did Jesus do? He began to teach them, interpreting all of Scripture "concerning Himself." I wish I could have heard that message! Jesus knew that a more careful reading of Scripture would have helped the two to understand and get it right. From Scripture, Jesus told them how Christ had to suffer these things and then "enter into His glory." These two had missed that part and thus needed to continue to study Scripture. After their eyes opened to recognize who He was, their response was, "Were not our hearts burning within us while he talked with us ... and opened the Scriptures to us?" (Luke 24:13–35). After Jesus departed, the two disciples returned at once to Jerusalem to tell the others the truth they had learned.

Jesus used Scripture to paint a true picture of reality. He helped His disciples to understand missing information. This is our mission as teachers. In many cases, worldview integration provides missing or additional information that enhances our developing worldview.

Answering Questions

This book is not meant to answer all the questions nonbelievers have about Christianity; many great books have already done so.

Instead, this book is intended to introduce some of these issues for ongoing study and to provide a broad framework for answering difficult questions. Once a teacher begins to think in an integrated way, there is a natural hunger to develop a deeper understanding of other worldviews, often by reading apologetic material to help confirm and defend the Christian worldview. This was true for me, and I hope it will be true for others as well. The Christian community is in need of true biblical thinking.

If there is just one biblical worldview (God's true perspective) and we all are limited humans as we pursue it, then it behooves us to submit our thinking continually to Scripture. We may be holding inconsistent beliefs or be expressing those beliefs in unbiblical ways. Both teacher and students are subject to continued study of Scripture. Biblical integration is an opportunity for teachers and students to continue growing and refining their worldview by bringing it into *conformity to God's view of things.*

In *Naming the Elephant,* James Sire wrote:

> Every fiber of my being cries out for a worldview that is not just my own story, my own set of propositions, my own interpretation of life, but one that is universally, objectively true, one in which the really real is the God Who Is There, and in which human beings are truly made in His image and capable of knowing at least some of "the way things actually are." The Bible assumes that this sort of knowledge is possible and that it is the major vehicle by which we can know what is the case, not just about the world but about this God Who Is There.... "All men by nature desire to know," said Aristotle. Yes, and in a postmodern world we have to add, "All of us desire to know the truth, not just a story constructed by ourselves." (2004)

To that I say, amen! The book Sire alluded to, *The God Who Is There* by Francis Schaeffer, is a personal favorite of mine. In it, Schaeffer addressed the oncoming changes in the way humans come to know truth, which he called "the most crucial problem ... facing Christianity today" (1968).

Youth from Christian homes were being confused because "they do not understand the alternatives with which they are being presented." A challenge to the existence of absolutes was on the rise. The first principle of classical logic—"A is not non-A"—was being abandoned.

Schaeffer wrote that assessment more than 40 years ago. The chickens have now come to roost. His description of the barriers to developing a Christian worldview was a challenge to me as a young teacher. It is much more of a challenge today.

Implications for the Classroom

When teachers desire to promote the development of a *biblical* worldview, it is not sufficient to tell students, "This is true, I have found it so in my own experience. Just trust me." Students who really like the teacher might outwardly give assent to the teacher's worldview instruction, but inwardly think, "Well, that is your truth; I have mine." Some will think, "My ideas are filled with love, and God is love and so my ideas are truth."

I conclude this chapter by imploring Christian educators to consider developing a biblical worldview *with* your students as you, and they, design research and processing activities that go to Scripture for answers. When clear answers related to the subject area under study cannot be found, hold an open mind and continue to search for truth *together*. We need a common standard rather than our "own truth." We have it in the Bible, but it takes hard work to prepare learning activities that will connect to and distinguish from a biblical view.

Eleven

A Pedagogical Model for Worldview Integration

Having looked at the nature of worldview thinking and some of the alternative systems of thought, we now address *how* to teach worldview thinking in a Christian educational setting. I have found over the years that presenting a model or approach to guide the actual design of the curriculum for integration of a biblical worldview has been helpful to teachers who have never tried anything other than prayer and occasional devotionals for their "biblical integration."

The teaching model addressed in this book was developed over several decades. After obtaining my master's degree, I returned with my family to Philadelphia, where my husband had accepted a faculty position at Philadelphia College of Bible (now Cairn University). I scheduled an interview at the local public school. However, the day of the interview I received a call from my pastor, who had started a Christian school several years earlier in response to the court cases that removed prayer and Bible reading from public schools.

The administrator of the Christian school had contracted a serious illness and the school board wanted an assistant principal/part-time teacher to be available in case someone was needed during the school year.

I took the job and found myself in a Christian school setting instead of a public school. All of my basic education had been in public schools, so I was at a disadvantage in trying to distinguish what a Christian school should really look like. After about three weeks, I asked myself, "What should I be doing differently here than I would be doing if I had taken the job at the public school?" I knew that parents wanted prayer and Bible reading in class, but there had to be something more. That question led to the development of the model for biblical integration shared in this book.

I considered myself an integrated person. At Wheaton College, I had been required to read everything Francis Schaeffer had written up to that time. I used that experience as well as my Bible knowledge (acquired formally at Cairn University, and informally in individual and group study) to develop my own biblically informed worldview. I knew how important it was to be whole in thought and actions, in scholarship, and in community. I wanted to live an undivided life, wholeheartedly committed to Christ, but I did not know how to help my students do the same. I wanted to affect a kind of learning that would lead to a coherent, biblical view of life and learning. I wanted to teach in such a way that students would consciously connect math with science, science with the language arts, literature with the social sciences—and all of learning to the integrating core of biblical truth. I found that student processing activities opened up opportunities for worldview integration, so I was on my way.

The more I interrelated subject matter, the more opportunities I had for worldview integration. While teaching a sixth grade class, I found a suggestion in the teacher's edition of the textbook to have students research the similarities between the Piltdown Man and the Cardiff Giant. I sent my students to the library to read the "Piltdown Man" entries in the archived 1950 *Columbia Encyclopedia* and the current *World Book Encyclopedia*. In the old encyclopedia, the Piltdown Man was reported as the missing link science had been looking for since Darwin's day. The new *World Book* declared the Piltdown finding to be a hoax like the Cardiff Giant. The Piltdown hoax had been believed by the scientific community for more than 40 years.

In comparing and contrasting the two stories, students learned about scientific hoaxes and began to understand that ongoing investigation and advances in technology make science open to change. We compared the concept of "change" in science knowledge to the unchangeableness in the Word of God. Students listed some of the major scientific questions addressed in the Bible, as well as the natural phenomena that are not. This led to a wonderful discussion of whether the answers to all questions can be found in the Bible.

This experience propelled me into a lifelong project. I looked at every enrichment and expansion activity in the curriculum guide, seeking opportunities to integrate the lesson with a biblical worldview. It took the next five or six years to begin to develop the model shared here.

Models for Integration in Christian Schools

Before developing a worldview model or approach to biblical integration, several other approaches that are practiced today must be addressed. I have observed three models in Christian academic settings: the Interpersonal/Spontaneous Model, the Parallel Model, and the Integrating Core Model.

The Interpersonal/Spontaneous Model

"Oh yes, I biblically integrate. Anytime a student has a question that relates to both the subject and the Bible, I answer it using a little sermon or devotional. You really don't need to *plan* for integration if you are an integrated person. Opportunities just pop up!"

This model assumes that the teacher is an integrated person who will consciously look for the teachable moments and spontaneously integrate as content promotes questions and connections. There are no curricular activities *planned* in the lesson.

This approach is indeed necessary, but not sufficient for the Christian school or for any school wishing to have an integrated curriculum. Recall the conclusions Chubb and Moe recorded in *Politics, Markets, and America's Schools*. They concluded that private schools can be much more intellectually coherent than public schools due to their mission. Private schools do not superimpose ad hoc value collections, but rather values that "constitute an integrated whole." This is accomplished, according to the researchers, through the "strategic *design of their curriculum*." Spontaneity is good—but planning is essential!

The Parallel Model

"I teach social studies, not Bible. Spiritual knowledge is for the family and the religion teacher. Of course, I begin most classes with prayer. It's a great way to get the kids quiet!"

The Parallel Model reflects the belief that there are two or more revelations from God that speak *equally* with authority in their own realm. Two tracks operate in curriculum planning, but they never cross. These two might be called secular knowledge and sacred knowledge. Sometimes the two tracks are referred to as faith and reason (as though there is no faith involved in secular knowledge and no reason in sacred knowledge).

It is true that the content of God's revelation to humankind in His Word and in His world does not need to be "integrated" in and of itself as knowledge; however, the human mind needs to be integrated. It is constantly influenced by worldview answers that come from the culture. Therefore, our minds must be continually informed by a biblical view of things.

The two-track approach never brings together subject matter and God's revealed Word; it is not integration at all. A Christian school that operates using this model will often require their teachers to pray (and perhaps read a portion of the Bible) before class to "integrate" school learning. These schools might have a separate religion class to take care of the one track. Many parochial schools function under this model.

Although there is an acknowledgment of both general and special revelation, and of both faith and reason in the process of knowing, and there is an understanding of the importance of moral or religious values that include prayer and the Bible, there is no planned attempt to bring these sources of knowledge and ways of knowing together into a larger whole. Furthermore, there is little attempt to settle the issue of what happens when there is clear conflict between knowledge sources. The parallel model is inadequate for the development of an integrated worldview. This model leads to a dualism that is damaging to the human personality.

The Integrating Core Model

> "I plan for worldview integration just like I plan the curriculum for other important learning outcomes. I find that using subject-to-subject integration and some of the suggested enrichment activities often helps me to design activities that help the students process new material in light of biblical answers to life's biggest questions. Biblical truth is the integrating center."

The third model is the one developed in this book. I have used this model for more than 35 years. In this model, one begins with a set of *examined* worldview beliefs (not just Christian clichés or stories learned in Sunday school). These core beliefs are biblical truths that address life's biggest questions. The teacher must intentionally look for natural opportunities to *connect* or *distinguish*. The third task in this model is to move forward in continued study of the subject area and the Bible when confronted with difficult questions. Continued study moves the student and the teacher in a direction that will ultimately allow for integrative activities.

The teacher then plans student processing activities as an *integral part* of the lesson. Students are challenged to examine God's perspective on science, math, language arts, history, music, physical education, or literature. The teacher must assess learning just as he or she would assess any learning (looking for true development in the students, not just rote memorization of the teacher's lecture). This means writing a test question, preparing a project assignment or activity, or using a performance as an instrument to measure student understanding of worldview connections and distinction.

This model allows one to view life and learning as a unified whole. One's worldview beliefs can affect incoming knowledge, and incoming knowledge can affect one's worldview, so there must be student processing activities that help inform a growing biblical worldview and assessment. The activities serve to enhance and expand the appreciation and understanding of life and learning. One's rule for truth judging is developed. This model answers the question, "What do I do when there is clear conflict between knowledge sources? Am I secular or sacred on demand, or am I integrated with a Christian worldview?" Integrity is the goal!

Four Elements of a Worldview Approach to Biblical Integration:

There are four essential elements in the worldview model or approach to biblical integration.

1. Biblical answers to life's biggest questions—the worldview integrating core.

2. Engaging cognitive interactive lessons—regular curricular lesson plans that go beyond rote learning and rise above the drawing of personal conclusions without outside standards.

3. Student processing activities for worldview thinking—designed within the regular curriculum and connected, in a natural way, to the lesson or unit at hand.

4. Assessment of worldview thinking—designed to discover how the students are making sense of the answers to worldview questions that are posed in the lesson and helps the student, as well as the teacher, evaluate learning.

Biblical Answers to Life's Biggest Questions

This first element of the worldview approach, using questions to identify worldview perspectives, has been addressed in the first ten chapters of this book. The questions approach simplifies the process of biblical integration and makes it manageable for teachers.

The university students I teach use the basic issues in philosophy to formulate questions.

Some graduate students, and perhaps some Christian school teachers who have not had a prerequisite philosophy course, may find such an approach more intimidating than using the questions in *The Universe Next Door* by James Sire. Select the format you wish to use.

One very effective activity is to read and chart the eight worldviews outlined in Sire's book and compare each one to Christian theism. While these questions provide an excellent framework, they are not exhaustive. There are sub-questions under these eight questions.

1. What is really real? What is prime reality?

2. What is the nature of external reality, the world around us?

3. What or who is a human being?

4. Is there life after death? What happens to a person at death?

5. How do we know? Why is it possible to know at all?

6. What is the basis for morality? How do we know what is right and wrong?

7. What is the meaning of human history?

8. What are the life implications and commitments related to my accepted beliefs?

A teacher who wishes to design integrative activities in the curriculum must not only examine biblical answers to worldview questions, but also be aware of other worldview answers that may appear in textual material. Using key worldview questions makes the task more manageable.

One additional consideration when developing this element of the worldview model is the nature or structure of each subject area. Structure includes the methods of inquiry, big ideas, and the standard for truth-judging in a particular discipline. According to learning theorist Jerome Bruner, understanding the structure of the subject is helpful in relating it to other things. Writing about structure, Bruner said that we understand better when we understand structure because it simplifies the process of *relating or connecting* information to other things we know. "Grasping the structure of a subject is ... understanding it in a way that permits many other things to be related to it meaningfully. To learn structure, in short, is to learn how things are related" (1977). There is a relationship between the nature of the subject and attempts to integrate that subject with other subjects and worldview questions.

Because I had taught math and science in middle school, it was relatively easy for me to determine the particular worldview questions they addressed. My university students (who are preparing to teach health and physical education, science, English, reading and the language arts, mathematics, the arts, social studies, and history) find the task fairly easy in their own subject areas. Elementary level educators are required to understand the structure of more than one or two subject areas, so this activity is more challenging for them. Graduate students have little difficulty with the task because they have been teaching their material for years, and are therefore very familiar with the content and domain-specific skills to be learned.

Consider how the structure of science relates to the question, "What is the nature of the external world?"

Science by its nature is:

- *Orderly.* Humans can measure and make predictions, determine probabilities, and use discoveries to function in the world. God created humankind with the capacity to make discoveries concerning natural phenomenon, measure findings, make predictions, and use this knowledge. He commanded humans to subdue and have dominion over the earth.

- *Knowable.* Truth is found by exploring natural phenomenon using the senses and reason. Humans, although limited by their senses and fallible reasoning, can discover truth. Scientific knowledge is always open to investigation and change. Therefore, what is considered truth in science today may be proved to be false upon further investigation. Change in science knowledge is inevitable as more study is carried out. Truth in science is absolute (God knows every law or pattern or principle we will discover) but it is not known absolutely by humans because of the limits of our senses and reasoning capacities. Therefore, what is considered truth in science today may be proved incomplete or false upon further investigation.

- Science can speak to more than just the nature of the external world.

- What is ultimate reality, the starting point of all that exists? *God.*

- How did the cosmos come to exist? Did it have a beginning? Is the world designed and created? Who designed and created the cosmos? Is the cosmos chaotic or orderly? Does it reflect intelligence or happenstance? *God designed and created the cosmos.*

- How does the world function and how is it sustained? What are the processes built into nature that provide for life? What is the role of God in the process? What is the role of human beings in the process? *God sustains His creation.*

- Who or what gets the credit for creation and for how it is sustained? *God sustains the cosmos, and we owe Him thanks.*

Understanding the structure of a subject area—its method of inquiry and truth-judging, its basic conceptual framework and big ideas—is vital to integrative learning. Appendix Four contains further illustrations about the value of this practice.

Conclusion

The first element in the worldview approach to biblical integration is a clear understanding of worldviews, what integration means in the curriculum, and what is being integrated. Previous chapters have dealt with these concepts. The underlying structure of the subjects you teach is also of great importance. The last three elements in the model will focus not so much on *what* the teacher is integrating, but *how* it is being integrated. The *how* is concerned with the nature of human beings and learning.

ACTIVITY

1. Why do you suppose that the first element in biblical worldview integration includes the examination of the educator's own worldview?

2. How do the terms *connecting* and *distinguishing* describe what worldview thinking is all about?

3. For biblical integration, why is it important to understand the structure of the subject(s) you teach?

Twelve

Engaging Cognitive Interactive Lessons

Marsha: "I try to use best practices in my classroom and for me those come from cognitive learning approaches."

Alex: "I tried some of those methods after graduating from university, but they just don't work in my subject areas. I teach Bible and history and these two subjects just lend themselves to a more telling model."

Marsha: "I am not talking about methods we use. I'm talking about using an approach to teaching that fits with an understanding of how humans learn."

Alex: "But what about Bible, Marsha? Don't those cognitive approaches just lead to students pooling their ignorance without biblical knowledge? Is that real learning?"

This chapter addresses some of the fallacies and misunderstandings related to human learning, including the learning of various subject areas. It is true that some teachers excuse their subjects from an approach derived from learning theory because they think that the subject they teach is outside the bounds of the theory. However, the innate nature of human learning remains the same, at every level and in every subject area. I mention this misconception because some view biblical integration as primarily Bible teaching. Where the Bible is concerned, teachers sometimes abandon their well-developed theory of learning and revert to "preaching" or "sharing." With the above in mind, the next two chapters address how all humans learn, regardless of age level or subject.

How Do Humans Learn?

Cognitive interactive learning theories attempt to explain how humans learn. Just as behaviorism claimed to be the first true scientific theory of learning because it uses observable behaviors as data, cognitive interactive theory also claims to be scientific because it, too, uses observable behaviors as evidence for cognition and learning.

Answers to the age-old question of how humans learn are offered by learning theorists of various persuasions. Their research and conclusions are promoted in educational psychology books studied in schools of education. Some teachers, however, have not examined the major questions about the nature of human learning, nor have they been encouraged to inform their understandings using a biblical perspective. Therefore, they may be easily swept away by every new "theoretical panacea" that comes along, or they may become cynical and close-minded to new research and new ideas altogether. Neither option is very productive.

What follows is designed to stimulate serious thinking about the question of how humans learn in order to promote effective teaching. "What is a human being?" and "How do humans learn?" are themselves worldview questions that should be integrated with one's Christian beliefs as an educator. It is a part of one's instructional philosophy.

Teachers who have read and studied in the current field of learning theory might have conversations in the teacher's lounge that sound like this.

Marge: "What do you think about the article on integrative teaching and constructive learning? I don't think I can buy into this approach. New fads like constructivism and integrative learning really champion the *processes* of knowing and ignore the content."

Jason: "Really? I thought the focus in the article was on something being 'constructed' by the mind as it interacts with incoming information. Materials or *content* are needed for construction of meaning. Aren't they?"

Marge: "I guess so, but the theory is all about what students do in coming up with their own personal knowledge and not about the material to be learned. There are no standards other than the personal constructions of the learner. I thought that the theory was totally anti-Christian anyway. And anyway, our subject matter curriculum committee will be out of work."

Tamara: "That may not be so bad. I'm on that committee! Look, anyone can use constructivist, behaviorists, humanist, or whatever, methods. You don't have to buy into the theory behind it. Theories are schemes of understanding, not methods."

Jason: "You may be right, Tamara. The article is addressing theory and just adds some methods for illustrations. Anyway, I thought that constructivism was a theory of learning rather than a theory of teaching."

Tamara: "I am a teacher; I just use what works! This fad will blow over just like the last ten! Remember when the principal made us all try the flipped classroom?"

The issue under review in the teacher's lounge reflects some confusion related to the nature of cognitive interactive learning. Broadly speaking, constructive theories stand in stark contrast to reactive theories such as behaviorism. Constructivism, on the other hand, is a constructive theory that holds to an underlying set of beliefs that address the nature of the human learner *and* the nature and source of knowledge. Constructivism's theory of knowledge and implications for learning are the problem for many Christians today. Constructivism weds psychology and philosophy, and as such must be examined by Christian educators.

In *Psychology and the Human Dilemma*, psychologist Rolo May comments that, "The critical battles between approaches to psychology ... will be on the battleground of the image of man—that is to say, on the conceptions of man, which underlie the empirical research." May was a humanistic existentialist who, at the time of his writing, argued that the field of psychology had not understood human beings as persons. His worldview placed humankind in the center of existence; however, he clearly understood that a major issue in the field of psychology was the nature of human beings. His view fit with humanistic theory. Underlying all theories of learning are beliefs about human nature and learning.

One's philosophy of education is not a matter of picking and choosing, but of intentionally forming answers to the basic questions of life that are related to human learning. One's theory of learning, however, is based upon both the underlying philosophical foundations and the theoretical research. In learning theory, however, rejecting what does not fit with one's worldview is a common practice. Lack of understanding the nature of theories has caused many to reject research because of the underlying beliefs of the researchers. This would be very much like rejecting a scientific finding just because the researcher is an atheist.

Why Study Theories of Learning?

Learning theories lead to *teaching* theories and ultimately to teacher practices in the classroom. Instructional choices come from somewhere. One's underlying beliefs should be operative in evaluating the new research or innovation. For the Christian, decisions about overall approaches to teaching and new applications should be informed by their Christian view of the nature of humans and knowledge. Current views should not be ignored just because the researchers extended some of the findings to fit their worldview. Instead, the believer brings an open mind to the task of connecting and distinguishing what fits with a biblical view and what does not. They ask, "What would this theory look like if my underlying assumptions were biblical rather than those held by the researcher?" This, in my view, is the way to continue to grow as educators. Teachers who are serious about building their work upon a solid foundation will not be satisfied with practices that contradict their beliefs. Nor will they throw out the baby with the proverbial bath water.

Constructive theories, as opposed to reactive theories, offer an approach to learning that should be explored. They present both potentials and problems. Cognitive interactive theorists see the stimulus-response reactive theory of the behaviorists as incomplete because of the assumptions related to human beings and learning. Behaviorists view humans as products of a mechanistic process of cause and effect; thus, teaching is an activity of conditioning from the outside. Outside factors, especially the teacher/conditioner, are the most important in the learning event. On the other hand, cognitive theorists believe that the human is born with a capacity to process incoming information and construct meanings. Something *inside*, as well as something outside, is important! In worldview integration, as in any teaching event, the focus is on learners and how they come to know *by nature*.

Cognitive Interactive Learning

Western educators have disagreed for nearly 100 years as to whether the learner is autonomously *active* or psychologically *passive* in the learning event.

Today, most educational articles address the problems in education as being related to passive versus active learning approaches. An emerging perspective, which this book supports, considers the learner to be *interactive* by nature. Cognitive interactive theories take the view that something inside *and* something outside matter equally in the learning event!

Two Views of Human Learning

Educators bring their own worldviews to the study of instructional theory and practice.

Within the boundaries of these beliefs, serious educators examine and choose from among the practical options that fit with their worldview. Confusion may occur as teachers/practitioners read the literature. Below is an example taken from *Constructivist Teaching,* which may clarify some aspects of decision making but may also lead to some confusion in deciding applications.

> Deciding about constructivist teaching, or deciding about any instructional procedure, is a matter of examining possible instructional methods to determine which are consistent with one's beliefs. Research and theory are helpful in identifying ways to teach. But teachers need to decide for themselves which techniques they will and will not use. When reduced to their essential character, these decisions deal with *beliefs about students,* their human qualities and learning processes, and with *beliefs about knowledge,* its form and function.
>
> If the beliefs about students and knowledge embedded in the technique or practice match the beliefs the teacher has about the students and knowledge, the technique will be one that fits the teacher. In order to make decisions about constructivist teaching, *two views of students and two views of knowledge* are especially important (Zahorik 1995; emphasis added).

While clearly suggesting that teachers must be concerned about their beliefs related to human qualities and learning and beliefs about knowledge—essential issues in learning theory—the above quote limits the options to just two key views of each. However, there are at least three views. Morris Bigge and Samuel Shermis identify a third view of human nature and learning that may help to solve the war between active and passive learning. They suggest that the various interpretations of experimental research "stem from disagreements over the fundamental nature of human beings and their relationship to their environments and the nature of motivation and perception" (2004). They call this fundamental nature the "actional" nature. This is a philosophical issue, an underlying belief essential for developing a theory of learning. They affirm that a psychologist's philosophical leaning "may not only determine the kinds of experiments one conducts, but also may influence the conclusions one draws from the evidence that is secured through experimentation." It is wise, therefore, to discern the underlying assumptions of the researcher/theorist before adopting a whole system or pertinent applications related to research and conclusions. (A good treatment of the three possible views of the "actional" nature may be found in *Learning Theories for Teachers,* published by Allyn and Bacon.)

While learning theorists continue to argue over the philosophical issue of the inborn nature of human learning, teachers typically respond to new ideas and the suggested applications using their own background and practices. Here is a typical discussion at a faculty meeting.

Aaron: "Well, my goal is to teach children using their own promptings from within and their prior experiences. I teach kids!"

Zoe: "What do you teach them?"

Aaron: "I teach them to think!"

Zoe: "Think about what?"

Aaron: "Well, they are learning to learn."

Zoe: "Learning *what*? Look, if you elementary teachers taught kids concepts, rules, and skills, the basics of geography, the framework for history, the basic generalizations of science and the patterns and relationships in math, we middle school and high school teachers would not have to go all the way back to ground zero in our subjects when you send them to us!"

Aaron: "Maybe so, but if our focus was content, content, content like yours, we would be delivering a bunch of academic clones and psychologically stressed students! Kids are individuals. Personal development is the primary goal of education."

Notice the emphasis on *content* by one speaker and *processes* by the other. One reason a teacher may reject the notion of the *autonomously active* human is the lack of concern for content, information, and skill development in that view. Sometimes, rejection occurs because of current educational movements, such as the standards movement. On the other hand, rejection of the *passive* learner is often accompanied by the concern that passive approaches ignore what the student brings to the learning event as an active participant.

The Christian educator who has studied learning theory without being encouraged to critique theories in light of a Christian worldview may operate on two levels:

1. What they learned about human learning from secular courses and texts in college or through educational journals and professional development seminars.

2. Their Christian beliefs about humans in general and knowledge in particular.

This may lead to conflicting results in attempting to practice worldview thinking about human learning. It may also lead to a form of biblical integration that does not fit with how humans learn. The latter is my primary concern.

Teachers who use best practices based upon the best available research may be tempted to teach Bible using methods that look more like preaching. This conditions students to think that Bible teaching (and learning) is different from "regular" learning. Some may tacitly assume that with the Bible, "to know is to do." They may believe that the biblical ideas themselves will change thinking and behavior without necessarily being processed and understood. This was a popular theory of learning espoused by Johann Herbart in the nineteenth century. It is sometimes called the funnel approach: pour in the new information and it will automatically produce learning.

To-know-is-to-do learning missed one important aspect of learning: student processing and understanding. In Colossians 1:9b, the Apostle Paul prayed for the Christians at Colossi to learn the word of God a certain way: "We continually ask God to fill you with the knowledge of his will through all the wisdom and *understanding* that the Spirit gives ..." Paul did not omit the concept of "understanding." Nor was this concept foreign to Jesus as He gave the parable of the sower in Matthew 13. Lack of understanding led to poor soil. The good soil produced well because of *understanding*. Student understanding is at the heart of cognitive theories. Learning is more than a reactive process. Students have a capacity to process and understand.

An Instructional Philosophy

The two primary views concerning the nature of the human and learning have arisen as corollaries to the two broad philosophical camps of the Enlightenment (scientific, mechanical, deterministic views that champion objective knowledge) and Romanticism (freedom, choice, personal development, and human flourishing views that champion the inner construction of knowledge). I argue that there may be a way to reconcile the two by understanding human learning as *interactive*.

Bigge and Shermis, describing actional nature, wrote:

> Furthermore, as used here, *innate* and *basic* are synonymous adjectives; both mean "original" or "unlearned." Consideration of the basic nature of people would be quite simple were there but one answer. But, interestingly, there are several distinctly different and mutually opposed answers to this question, each enjoying a good deal of support. (2004)

Those who hold that humans are *active* in their actional nature believe that underlying psychological characteristics are inborn; learning comes from forces inside the person. Learning is chiefly developmental. The environment is simply a location for natural "unfoldment" (the romantic/humanist tradition). Those who hold that humans are basically *passive* in their actional nature believe that human characteristics are determined primarily by the environment (the behaviorist tradition).

Those who hold that humans are interactive in actional nature do not equate learning with the unfolding of internal patterns, nor with an external conditioning process in which the learner is entirely passive. They believe that psychological characteristics arise as humans take in and make sense of information from an outside world.

This theory has, at times, been confused with one of the other two views or incorrectly labeled a combination of them. Neither is the case.

Process and Content

Cognitive interactive theory assumes that the learner and the learning environment are *equally* important and work together *as a unit* in the learning event. The focus is on how humans *process* incoming *information*. Cognitive interactive theory should not be confused with constructivism (though it is a constructive theory). Constructivism focuses on construction *inside the learner*. In its radical version, there is no affirmation that an external world exists as separate from the knower, as Ernst von Glasersfeld suggests in *Radical Constructivism*:

> Radical constructivism... replaces the notion of "truth" (as true representation of an independent reality) with the notion of "viability" within the subjects' experiential world. Consequently, it refuses all metaphysical commitments and claims to be no more than one possible model of thinking about the only world we can come to know, the world we construct as living subjects. (1995)

The beliefs inherent in this quote are why many Christian educators reject constructivism as a system and swing back to behaviorism. Some constructivist thinking is a bit more palatable, however. Some theorists, such as Bigge and Shermis, take a noncommittal attitude toward an independent reality; one need not affirm or deny a world that exists independent of the experiencing learner when developing a purely psychological system. These theorists focus on what the learner psychologically makes of incoming information. In contrast, a unified theory would affirm both the capacity to process information *and* environmental factors. These operate *as a unit* in the learning event. The interactive view not only allows for inside processing of information but also outside standards and competencies for assessment—a more practical, realistic view, in my opinion, for practicing educators who must assess learning. This view fits better with a biblical view of knowledge than the other two views.

The Christian worldview does not permit us to deny or ignore the external world and outside standards for truth; therefore, constructivism is not valid to adopt as a whole system of thinking. However, in rejecting this theory, some have failed to give the cognitive interactive theory that birthed constructivism a fair hearing. This may be one reason some have not used the research and conclusions of the emerging interactive theory and have slipped back into the use of passive models, especially for Bible and Bible-related teaching.

Interactive Teaching in Worldview Integration

If the development of a worldview is grasping answers to life's biggest questions, then developing a worldview informed by a biblical view is a building process that includes renovation (tearing down unbiblical understandings) and reconstruction (building a framework using biblical input). The process is inside the learner but uses an outside standard. The standard is a blueprint for the renovation.

Cognitive interactive learning is a theoretical framework for human learning that acknowledges internal and external factors *equally* in the learning event. This view offers an alternative to the approach of either humanistic theory (which posits that the human is psychologically *active* and focuses on inside factors) or behaviorism (which holds that the human is psychologically *passive* and focuses on outside factors). Here is a brief overview of the two perspectives.

Behaviorism

Behaviorism, which dominated much of the twentieth century and is alive and well today, holds that the human actional nature is *passive* and that learning happens because of outside factors (e.g., the teacher, textbook, DVD, or Internet). The learning model derived from this belief is one of outside stimuli soliciting a response followed by reinforcement. Future responses—the learning—are determined by the skilled conditioner/teacher and environmental reinforcement. *Outside forces trump anything inside the learner.* The model is very teacher-centered. Methods for teaching are primarily impressive (listening and reading).

Although some behaviorists grew in their knowledge and changed positions after the cognitive revolution had taken hold in America, B. F. Skinner, the best-known contributor to behaviorism, never changed his mind. When interviewed by David Goleman for the

New York Times in 1987, Skinner said, "The cognitive revolution is a search inside the mind for something that is not there. You can't see yourself process information; information processing in an inference from behavior—and a bad one, at that." Skinner's stimulus-response approach to learning led to an overall teaching model that revolved around the teacher: the teacher lectures, expects students to take notes exactly as given, expects exact answers as given in the notes, and reinforces the lesson afterward. This approach, although kind to subject matter content, missed the processing needed for effective learning and especially for worldview integrative learning.

The behavioristic model is still used today in many countries that were impacted by American education in the early 1900s. In some, the behavioristic approach is now considered their educational culture. When teaching a course in theories of learning in other countries, I try to help my students understand that the actional nature refers to the *innate* way humans learn. Methods are often cultural, but they must be used with an understanding of human nature in order to make learning easier and more natural.

This is not a purely Western idea. When teaching in Pacific Rim countries, I lead my students in exploring ten incidents in which Jesus promoted learning in His disciples. As we look at these teaching events, we ask why Jesus taught the way He did. Students look for and infer His understanding of the actional nature of the student and determine which of the basic natures (active, passive, or interactive) He seemed to embrace. The students have little difficulty in concluding that Jesus knew how humans learn—after all, He created us— and they invariably select the interactive nature to defend.

Humanistic Theory

Humanist theorists that follow the views of the eighteenth century Romantic naturalists believe that the human actional nature is autonomously *active* and that learning occurs primarily because of inside factors naturally unfolding. Learning is autonomous and developmental. *Inside factors trump anything outside.* The model for teaching is child-centered rather than subject-centered. Methods for teaching are primarily expressive (speaking and writing.) Friedrich Froebel, the "father of the kindergarten," believed humans unfold like a flower. He said: "All the child is ever to be and become, lies—however slightly indicated—in the child, and can be attained only through development from within, outward" (1908). The purpose of teaching and instruction is to bring ever more out of the child rather than to put more and more in.

A teaching approach for humanistic theory would stress activity. Student interest and needs guide activities as the child unfolds; students learn through their own prompting; student activities involve the student in their own learning and development. The approach focuses on student enjoyment and fun; feelings and emotions are central. Because students are naturally motivated, there is no need to motivate, and the classroom environment is simply a location for student activity.

Teachers who hold to the humanistic theory tend either to ignore their overall teaching approach while doing the "Christian" part of the curriculum, or to make the biblical integration simply God-words or feelings about Jesus with little content. Neither are worthy of a Christian school education.

For the Christian, content is vital in biblical integration. This is one of the reasons so many revert back to a behavioristic approach for biblical integration even if they use another approach in other subjects. This mistake can be avoided when one understands human learning as a cognitively *interactive* process. When one understands *how humans learn* as a cognitively interactive process, both content and processing are vital!

A Caution

> "Well, sometimes students are *passive* when I am talking and they are listening and other times they are *active* when they are doing something, or *interactive* when talking to one another. Don't you think they can be all three but at various times?"

This teacher is referring to *methods* that are physically active or passive or socially interactive rather than referring to *the way the mind works in the learning event*. The Christian educator must be alert to this common confusion regarding cognitive interactive learning: some equate it with physical or social methods rather than how the mind comes to know. Ask any group of teachers to identify which of the statements below fit with their idea of interactive learning.

1. Cooperative learning groups using project and discussion methods

2. A class discussion where all are involved together

3. Time for questions is planned into the lesson

4. Creative activities planned by the teacher

5. Technology in the classroom

6. A lecture to 500 in a lecture hall

Many teachers will identify all but number six as representing interactive learning. However, all of the above are methods! The *mind* is interactive when learning, even during a lecture, and will try to process incoming information (unless students have been trained to shut down and take notes when the teacher "tells"). Some human minds that have been so conditioned work this way in school but not at home, on the playground, at lunch, and in other life settings. Students who have been schooled under behavioristic theory must be reeducated to learn as they were created to learn.

In learning theory, "interactive nature" connotes more than a balance between passive and active methods. It is certainly more than methods that allow students to talk. Inside factors and outside factors are viewed as a unified whole *in the learning event* while retaining their own separate existence. Standards for knowledge (and therefore feedback assessment) and how the student is conceptualizing and making sense of the information are equally important! Methodology always includes both impressive (listening and reading) and expressive activities (speaking and writing) in every lesson.

Selecting the Best View

Some educational philosophers of the last century sought a balance between inner and outer factors that was very helpful to educators. Lois LeBar, one of my favorite professors at Wheaton College, declared:

> Educators of our own day are striving to achieve a balance between inner and outer factors. They realize the inadequacies both of so-called poor traditional education that seemed satisfied if pupils could parrot back content just as it had been presented to them, and of progressive education that seemed content to provide experience without sufficient guidance by teachers or norms of value. (1958).

Dr. LeBar traced the concept of inner and outer factors all the way back to John Amos Comenius, a seventeenth century Czech Christian educator who is considered the Father of Modern Education.

While the "balance" approach (inner and outer) helped teachers design curriculum, it also left the door open for teachers to favor one focus over the other. There was no overall approach to teaching that was described as "interactive" based upon the three mutually opposing views of the actional nature that would, by definition, exclude favoring one over the other. Now there is.

Assuming that educators are interested in examining various views of human nature and learning before committing to a teaching approach, how do they decide which theory of learning best fits with their views of human nature and learning? Teachers must come to a place of tentative confidence that what they are adopting fits best with their Christian worldview. Learning theory is a science and as such is open to change. Teachers must be open to lifelong learning in their field.

Here are some things for educators to consider. Does the educator believe that the human is a set of highly organized material, non-purposive and determined by the natural laws of cause and effect? This leads to the belief that humans are passive in the learning event. Does the educator believe that the human is an autonomous chooser who makes his own world and creates his own reality and knowledge out of his own private being as he develops? This view leads to the belief that the human is autonomously active in the learning event. The answers offered by the interactive view are an alternative. The view that the human being is interactive in actional nature might be adopted for various reasons and from divergent sources. However, an illustration out of the author's own perspective and the perspective of this book may be informative.

My first inclination as a teacher was to move away from behaviorism and toward humanistic theory because of the focus on the human being as special. Behaviorism made learning mechanical, manipulative, and dehumanizing for the very creatures God had created to learn. It was not long, however, until my studies led me to question the autonomy of the student and the lack of focus on content found in the approach that emerged from the autonomously active human. Dr. LeBar's focus on inner and outer factors was a rich part of my educational background as I was searching for answers.

In *A Christian View of Men and Things,* Gordon Clark concluded that "God has fashioned both the mind and the world so that they harmonize" (1981). Clark's view does not suggest that we can know reality perfectly, but it does suggest that a knowable world exists outside the human mind. Truth can be known in spite of human limits.

Furthermore, humans may understand correctly, partially, or incorrectly. Ongoing assessment, new information, and opportunities to change are vital in learning. The cognitive interactive view, with its robust focus on both internal and external factors, leaves room to preserve the concept that reality/objects exist outside the knowing mind and can be processed for understanding and growth. In *Ten Philosophical Mistakes,* philosopher Mortimer Adler addressed the misconception that human knowing changes the thing known. "Truth is what it is to me" might be the mantra that follows that mistaken thinking. Adler declared, however, that "our knowing something in no way affects or alters the thing we know.... The knowable exists quite independently of the knower and is whatever it is whether it is known or not, and however it is known. The word that most of us use to signify the independent character of the knowledge is the word 'reality'" (1985).

The view of knowledge that affirms *both* an objective world and the innate capacity of a subject to know what exists outside the knowing mind fits best with a Christian worldview. Cognitive interactive theory champions the human capacity for processing and constructing meaning as essential elements in learning. But human knowledge can be wrong or incomplete, as demonstrated when their thinking is measured by an *outside standard*. Inside and outside factors matter!

ACTIVITY

Using the content of this chapter, critique the following statement.

"Well, sometimes students are *passive* when I am talking and they are listening and other times they are *active* when they are doing something, or *interactive* when talking to one another. Don't you think they can be all three but at various times?"

Thirteen

A Cognitive Interactive Model for Teaching

Those of us who are educators can thank (or blame) German philosopher and educator, Johann Friedrich Herbart, for the existence of lesson plans. He was the first to formalize the process. In some ways, he was ahead of his time in thinking about human learning. In his view, the mind uses the *known* to learn the *unknown*, similar to the popular concept of using prior knowledge to make sense of new knowledge. Herbart's view of human nature and learning, however, viewed the student as a *passive* recipient of information poured in by the teacher. To him, ideas were dynamic and active, not the mind of the student. He did not focus on the cognitive capacity of the student, but on the organization of information by the teacher.

Herbart's elements of a lesson plan were: Clearness, Association, System, and Method. These four steps became five when students brought Herbart's theory to America in the 1880s. Teacher thinking followed this line of preparation:

- *Prepare* the students to be ready for the new lesson.

- *Present* the new lesson.

- *Associate* the new lesson with ideas studied earlier.

- *Use examples* to illustrate the lesson's major points.

- *Test* students to ensure that they had learned the new lesson (Dunkel 1969).

In the model above, who does the thinking for the new lesson? The teacher! While the labels of this teaching/learning model could be used as labels for the Cognitive Interactive model described in the previous chapter, the learning theory behind the model would be very different and yield different results. Herbart's lesson plan was very content-centered rather than learning-centered.

A Learning Model Leads to a Teaching Model

Labels for a model, on their own, do not promote effective student learning. This is true of any human learning theory. Underlying beliefs about the nature of the student and knowing must be considered first. Too often teachers are given a template to use in preparing lessons without an understanding of the theory behind it.

A *learning* model conceptualizes how we think humans learn. A *teaching* model addresses what we think is the best way to promote learning; it is rooted in how we think humans learn. The development moves from human learning theory to a teaching model (based on the learning theory) to lesson plans (based on the teaching model).

Methods, in contrast to models, are the tools we use to work through the plan to promote learning. Methods are simply activities used in the learning event to carry out the elements of the lesson. (The term "activities" here refers to methodology rather than to learning theory or a teaching model.) Methods are usually described in terms of the language arts: listening, reading, speaking, and writing. Under these four categories are numerous specific methods from which to choose.

An understanding of the teaching event as equally utilizing inside and outside factors is vitally important in interactive human learning: what the student is thinking and processing is just as important as what the teacher is thinking and delivering! Thus, "student processing activities" (designed by the teacher, the curriculum writers, or both) are an important element of learning. The focus is on what the student is doing with the new material. To carry out this element of a good lesson, the teacher must include activities that require the *student* to manipulate new information. The activities help the student fit the new knowledge with their own meaning schemes, as well as clarify, comprehend, store, and retrieve it later. These activities also promote the joy of learning.

Lesson Objectives

Objectives should be written in terms of the student and what the student will be able to do to show *understanding of, and potential action related to the big idea* of the lesson and related facts. Because cognitive interactive theory uses student behaviors as evidence for learning, the objective for the big idea of a lesson is very important.

Lesson objectives become very important as teachers write *worldview* objectives for lessons that address worldview questions. Cognitive theorists focus on big ideas around which related facts are organized. Facts are important, but they are organized around concepts and categories. The lesson and unit always move from the whole (the big idea) to the parts (supporting facts) and back to the whole. (This is very much *unlike* behaviorism, which moves from part to part to part to part, assuming the student will consequently understand the big idea of the lesson.) Studying the whole and then the parts before returning to the larger whole enables more students to grasp the main idea and develop the concept or skill. A biblical worldview objective may be integrated into the big idea objective or written as a separate objective, but it *must* be articulated somehow. Writing objectives for a lesson keeps the teacher moving toward the targeted focus.

The Delivery Elements of a Good Cognitive Interactive Lesson

Elements (not necessarily steps) of a good cognitive interactive lesson include:

Motivation: Engaging the Mind of the Student

The teacher develops an *activity* to activate the student's mind toward the lesson at hand, engaging prior knowledge or prior experiences and creating questions or problems to be addressed. (Suitable activities are sometimes provided in the curriculum lesson materials.) A motivation activity opens the students' mind to the subject that will be addressed in the lesson. This activity may also enable students to be open to the thinking processes that *connect* and *distinguish* new knowledge from prior knowledge.

Motivation refers to something *inside* learners that moves or drives them toward or away from something. It is *directional*. The teacher is always trying to activate the student's mind toward the lesson at hand or to reactivate the mind of the student as the lesson progresses; for this reason, one lesson plan may contain more than one motivation activity. Re-motivation is especially necessary in lessons that extend over two or more days.

Teachers, then, motivate when they activate or reactivate the minds of students toward the lesson at hand. This is far more than simply getting students' attention. If a third grade teacher "motivates" students by offering an extra five minutes of recess if the students pay close attention during math class, what are the students really thinking about? Recess! Not the lesson at hand.

Concept or Skill Development

This element includes *activities* designed for the student to obtain new information in an organized, connected way. Often, educators think that the best way for students to obtain information is through teacher lecture, but in this day of technology and alternative media sources, there are many other ways. From home or the classroom, teachers can find YouTube videos, artwork, and music that enhance the lesson. Students can research on their own or with guidance from the teacher. There are more methods to obtain information today than ever before. We live in an information society. (Beware, however: not everything on the Internet is accurate.)

Lecture is just one method among many. Interactive lectures can involve the teacher "telling" for 10 minutes, then pausing for pair-sharing or a brief processing activity before continuing the lecture. I use interactive lectures most of the time in university classes.

Student Processing Activities

This third element has been called "closure" by some educators, but not always understood as more than concluding or closing the lesson. True closure is related to the German *gestalt* concept—to fit into a whole. Closure in a lesson is designed to help the students understand, make sense, and fit the new information into their scheme of meanings or modify previous learning that may not fit with the new learning. (You may have studied the Cloze Procedure, which omits every "nth" word from a piece of reading. The reader tries to read the passage by filling in the words that have been left out; if the word the reader inserts makes sense grammatically and conceptually, the student is reading for understanding rather than just word-calling. They are making sense as a whole.)

Processing activities are designed to help students fit new information into their meaning schemes in a way that can be related to other knowledge. The activities in this element are always *student activities* designed to relate new information to old, to fit in or change prior thinking with new information, or to practice new concepts or skills.

When a student processing activity is done by an individual rather than a pair or group, it often serves as a formative assessment as well. A processing activity that is not used in day one of a lesson but planned as part of the entire lesson may be used as a re-motivation activity for day two. Student processing activities are needed for any lesson to promote effective learning. However, student processing activities are *essential* when using a worldview approach to biblical integration. This is one of the reasons for introducing this particular teaching model.

Assessment and Evaluation of Learning

The *activities* used for assessment come in two types: formative and summative. Formative assessments are included in each lesson; summative assessments may be administered after the concepts and skills have been formed to see if the information "stuck." Often, a unit will end with a summative test or project to guide the teacher's evaluation of the student's composite learning. The evaluation is a judgment based upon certain criteria and address how well the student met the criteria established for the unit. Most summative evaluations are graded and often weighted in value.

Formative assessments, on the other hand, provide feedback to students and teachers before a final test, project, or performance.

They are not always graded. The teacher and the students are assessing whether the student is getting the concept or developing the skill. The student should use the feedback to determine the need for more study time, request help, or determine to be patient and persist. The teacher may use the information from formative assessments for individual tutoring or for adjusting the next day's lesson. Regular formative assessment is vital to learning and promotes student effort.

Contrasting the Cognitive Interactive Model with Active and Passive Models

The chart below compares and contrasts the theories addressed earlier. As mentioned, the three views (active, passive, and interactive) are mutually opposed terms that indicate the way humans learn by nature—because they are humans. An educator can hold to just one of the three. Would each of these learning theories include all of these elements on a lesson plan?

Learning Theory	Behavioristic Theory	Humanistic Theory	Cognitive Interactive Theory
Actional nature	Student is cognitively *passive.*	Student is autonomously *active.*	Student is *cognitively interactive.*
Motivation	NO No need to motivate since nothing inside is important to the learning event. Get physical attention of the students by any means necessary.	NO No need for a *motivation or engagement* activity; students, by nature, are already motivated. The classroom is a location for inside prompts to unfold.	YES *Motivation* is an essential element because something inside the learner matters in learning.

New Information	*YES* Students learn new information through a pattern of stimulus, response, and reinforcement. Lesson plan is filled with content to be learned.	*NO* New information planned by the teacher is not a focus and usually not a specific target. Discussion topics often come from the students themselves.	*YES* Content is very important and must be carefully planned. Something outside the learner matters.
Student Processing Activities	*NO* There is no need; nothing inside matters; find the behavior you want or arrange the environment to get the behavior you want and then reinforce those behaviors.	*YES* Lesson plan stresses *activity*; the goal is learning in general, not learning a particular set of content. Physical activity is often thought to be the key to personal learning as students develop.	*YES* Lesson plan must have student processing activities, not just physical activities, although physical and social activities often enhance mental processing. The focus is content that is processed and understood by the student.
Assessment/ Evaluation	*YES* Information is given back in the words of the teacher and the notes as given. Teacher reinforces right answers.	*NO* There may be a personal assessment of how the student feels about the activities or a conclusion of what is personally learned, but there is no assessment based upon objective information. The teacher may determine that the kids are learning to learn or developing their innate ability to think.	*YES* Students must know whether or not they understand the material, and the teacher needs to know that as well. Assessment is feedback for continued learning and very important. There are standards outside the learner by which to measure learning.

Notice that the responses for behavioristic theory and humanistic theory are diametrically opposed in most cases. Cognitive interactive theory addresses the elements found in the other two and adds one other: motivation.

Relating the Cognitive Interactive Teaching Model to Biblical Worldview Integration

Worldview integrative activities must allow for student processing and internalization in which students are led to compare, contrast, connect, relate, correct, distinguish, or continue researching subject matter. Biblical answers to life's biggest issues are explored as a regular part of the curriculum.

Biblical worldview answers are not just the teacher's or school's view, but God's. This is vital in this age of student mantras such as, "This is my truth!" and "That's truth to you, but this is truth to me." Young people ignore even beloved teachers when they begin to "preach." I have visited hundreds of classrooms in Christian schools and seen, over and over, that when a high school teacher gets to the end of a lesson and tacks on a spiritual analogy or devotional, the students stop taking notes ("This is not the important stuff") and often shift to a relaxed, disinterested posture. Students need to grapple with issues within the lesson itself and draw conclusions under the guidance of a teacher who knows and loves the Lord. This is best done via the cognitive interactive model.

Preparing for a worldview approach to biblical integration is preparing for a learning event, and as such, teachers must understand that the mind of the student must be engaged in learning and must process new information in light of previous knowledge. Processing activities are designed to help students draw conclusions for their own thinking and acting. It is hoped that incomplete or unbiblical answers will be challenged and the students will develop a disposition toward conforming their life views to God's view.

Since a teaching model based upon the interactive nature of the human being and learning is neither passive telling and testing nor unguided activity, but rather an orchestration of four basic elements, one might think like this:

1) *If something inside matters* in the learning of new information, I must plan to engage that inside something in order to activate prior knowledge and motivate learning the lesson at hand. What will I do or have the students do that will accomplish this goal?

       Result: Engage the mind (inside) toward the lesson at hand using an activity planned by the teacher (outside).

  Worldview thinking: If I know the worldview question addressed in the lesson and have planned for connecting or distinguishing a biblical view in the materials, I may wish to begin the thought processes of the students in the lesson motivation element of the lesson.

Example: For a lesson on constellations, I gave each of my middle school students an uncompleted dot-to-dot picture and asked them to complete the figure, name their picture, and write a brief story about it. Together we shared the names of their pictures (airplane, peeled banana, star fish with a broken leg, stealth bomber, etc.—all from the exact same outline). Then some of the students shared their short stories. Then I told them that hundreds of years ago in Mesopotamia, people looked up at the night sky and "connected the dots," forming pictures from the stars. I asked them to use the activity to define constellations. They read their definitions to one another. They were encouraged when they turned to the first page of the unit on constellations in their science book and compared their definitions to the definition in the text.

The students were certainly more engaged after this activity than they would have been if I had simply told them to turn to page 59 and find the definitions for constellations and asterisms.

The motivation activity helped to activate thinking to be used later in the unit for student processing—and worldview integration.

Later in the lesson I had the students *connect* the existence of constellations to the Creator (constellations are mentioned in the Bible several times by name) and to the biblical idea of the heavens declaring the glory of God (constellations are visible to every people group the world over). Seeing God's creativity and giving Him credit for what he has done is a basic form of worship in science class.

Later, I conducted a *distinguishing* activity by having the students study the human myths about the constellations and the difference between *astronomy* and *astrology*. In this worldview activity, they discovered why astrology is forbidden in the Bible. Students need to discover and process this and draw a conclusion for their own lives.

2) **If something outside matters,** I must study and organize content and skill development strategies to deliver these in light of the students' prior experiences, knowledge base, and current skill level. What will I do or have the students do that will accomplish the goal of having the students obtain new information? There will be times when a reading or research assignment or lecture will reference an article, quote, original document, historical or current event, or a story that can be used in later student processing activities. Sometimes these are right in the curriculum content or the teacher's suggested activities. Other times, the teacher may need to add them.

Result of thinking: *Provide new information* by *giving it* (outside the student) or creating a student activity that requires the student *to get* the new information from some outside source (textbook, original document, DVD, Internet, etc.).

Example: The previously mentioned activity of comparing the Cardiff Giant to the Piltdown Man. I used the two sets of information as an opportunity for worldview integration when we returned from our trip to the library. All I did was create a comparative activity and pose several questions.

3) **If learning occurs as information is taken in and processed by the individual,** I must create student processing activities that are designed to help the student make sense of new information, construct adequate understandings, and practice skills. What will I have the students do to promote this goal?

Result of thinking: *Create student processing activities* to help the student make sense out of new material or skill, form closure, make connections (with prior knowledge), generalize, draw conclusions, or practice and use a skill.

4) **If learning occurs inside and I must assess learning,** I must create ongoing assessment activities that indicate whether students are understanding. What will the students do to indicate their learning or to demonstrate growth in a skill?

Assessment is vital to worldview integration because integration itself occurs in the mind of the student. Worldview development should be assessed in the lesson and evaluated to "get the student-processing outside" (so the teacher can hear or see it) as a sampling of their understanding.

Result of thinking: *Assess learning* by using student expressions, in their own words, of inside processed understandings of the content addressed. For skill development, use the skill in some kind of performance to determine how well students understand the skill in context and can use it.

Conclusion

Teachers who are serious about promoting learning in their students will invite conversation about the potentials of cognitive interactive approaches. The cognitive interactive model is a model for every lesson in general but is especially helpful in preparing lessons that include worldview integrative activities. Appendix Three provides an outline of a Bible lesson using the cognitive interactive model.

ACTIVITY

Take a lesson you have taught or will teach and lay it out according to the template provided in this chapter. Look for places among the lesson elements in which biblical worldview integration might naturally fit.

Fourteen

Student Processing Activities and Critical Thinking

Although this book is about worldview integration and not learning theory per se, it must be stated that true integration cannot be accomplished in a classroom in which students are spoon-fed material rather than encouraged to process new knowledge. Learning is more than giving back notes in rote form for a test. This is why several chapters of this book are specifically designed to address the topic of human learning theory and applications. The last chapter offered a lesson template using the elements of a cognitive interactive approach to learning and teaching. This chapter continues to connect human learning to worldview integration.

Developing a Disposition Toward Biblical Worldview Integration

Teachers who utilize a teaching model such as the one presented in the last chapter are well on their way to the development of this approach to biblical integration. However, they must have a disposition toward adapting the curriculum for the purpose of worldview thinking. Teachers must understand the importance of having one's worldview informed by and conformed to God's view. As educators, we must understand that this is a *curricular* issue.

I often hear teachers comment that doing biblical integration will take too much time out of the curriculum and away from things that must be covered. This is a misunderstanding. The approach developed in this book does not take time from the curriculum; it makes the curriculum more robust and learning more coherent. Worldview integration is not an addition to the curriculum but an integral part of it. It promotes one of the current goals of the curriculum: the development of critical thinking. If we are serious about Christian education, we cannot afford to ignore biblical integration. But to further promote a disposition and to demonstrate that this approach is not outside the regular curriculum, this chapter will address worldview integration as the process of critical thinking, a common goal in education today.

The Process of Critical Thinking

In "The Thought-Filled Curriculum," Arthur Costa wrote, "Humans are born with the capacity and inclination to think. Nobody has to 'teach us how to think' just as no one teaches us how to move or walk" (2008).

Thinking is a natural internal mental process that uses information, new or prior, as input and integrates it into meaning schemes and previously learned information and experiences. Thinking is at the heart of human learning. A Christian view will note that thinking is related to our nature as image-bearers: we think because God thinks.

A classical definition of critical thinking, which has been commonly accepted for nearly 100 years, is "the examination and test of propositions of any kind which are offered for acceptance, in order to find out whether they correspond to reality or not" (Sumner 1940).

There is a *standard* for the critiquing process. Does the thinking about a proposition, a statement that can be judged true or false, correspond to what is the actual case? Correspondence to reality is the standard.

The National Council for Excellence in Critical Thinking uses the following definition:

> Critical thinking is the intellectually disciplined process of actively and skillfully conceptualizing, applying, analyzing, synthesizing, and/or evaluating information gathered from, or generated by, observation, experience, reflection, reasoning, or communication, as a guide to belief and action. (Scriven and Paul 1987; emphasis added)

Postmodernism and Critical Thinking

In our postmodern pop culture, critical thinking is understood as thinking that involves using your own knowledge or point of view to decide whether or not someone else's ideas are right or wrong. For example, Thomas and Thorne write:

> Another way to form ideas is to use critical thinking. This involves a person using his own knowledge or point of view to decide what is right or wrong about someone else's ideas. This is sometimes called "having a mind of your own." It means that a person doesn't have to believe or accept everything that someone else says or writes. (2009)

The last statement is certainly true about critical thinking. However, the standard is, "my own knowledge or point of view." No wonder there is little civil debate of ideas on TV talk shows. To express their own point of view, guests and hosts have to talk over one another rather than debating the idea with substance.

It is no wonder that those who hold to Sumner's classical definition are suspicious of the attempts to develop critical thinking in schools today. Many decry the blatant rejection of an external standard for knowledge. For example, one educational activist is strongly suspicious of school attempts at developing critical thinking in this postmodern culture and believes that "critical thinking is typically used to tell students that they should not trust conventional wisdom, tradition, religion, parents, and all that irrelevant, old-fashioned stuff. Critical thinking, somewhat surprisingly, also turns out to be highly contemptuous of facts and knowledge" (Deitrick Price 2015).

The word "critical" is closely related to two Greek words: *kriticos*, meaning discerning judgment, and *kriterion*, meaning standards. *Critical* thinking, therefore, involves the process of judging—a "critique"—and a criterion, or standard, by which to judge. These are two components of the methodology for a worldview approach to biblical integration, as well. Integrating is the process, and the standard for truth-judging is the set of biblical answers to life's biggest questions.

Wisdom and Critical Thinking

It may be apparent that the approach suggested in this book is considered to be, in part, critical thinking using biblical truth as the standard in developing a biblical worldview. One of the goals for Christian education has been to develop wisdom that begins "with the fear of the Lord"—a biblical view that refers to a set of applied content. Wisdom is an application or result of biblical worldview thinking and demands content as well as the process of sound thinking.

In *Wisdom, Intelligence, and Creativity Synthesized*, Robert J. Sternberg cautions, "Although knowledge is necessary for wisdom, it is not sufficient for it. Merely having knowledge does not entail its use in judging rightly, soundly, or justly" (2003). Indeed, wisdom demands the ability to *think critically and act wisely*.

Wisdom and right choices have often been seen as products of good thinking. Webster's New World College Dictionary defines wisdom as the "power of judging rightly and following the soundest course of action, based on knowledge, experience, understanding, etc." (2010).

In response to the early attempts to develop critical thinking, which separated the skill development from the regular curriculum, Robert J. Swartz wrote, "Teachers who have taken the time to understand critical thinking based on their own experience and study have turned away from prepackaged curriculums in favor of infusing critical thinking into the restructured content of their own teaching" (1986).

A worldview approach to biblical integration curricular issue and the integrative activities are infused into the content of teaching as a part of the regular curriculum, not just tacked on.

Essential Learning Activities for Worldview Integration

There are at least four different kinds of activities that help students to process and integrate a biblical worldview. These activities are always targeted toward answering one of the worldview questions or sub-questions.

Connection Activities

The student compares something in the curriculum that addresses a worldview question to a biblical answer to the same question. The activities involved in this category are designed to highlight similarities between a Christian worldview and the worldview answers given or implied in the curriculum.

Distinction Activities

The student contrasts something in the lesson materials to a biblical view. These activities include evaluation, judgment, and distinction of differences between the worldview in the material and a biblical view.

Continued Study Activities

When a question with no immediate answer arises, more study and research is needed. The teacher and students devise a plan to investigate the question; ideally, this will lead to integrative thinking even if tentative in nature.

Assessment Activities

Assessments provide feedback to discover whether or not the student can connect or distinguish their thinking in light of the integrating core.

Integration across and among subject areas provides greater opportunities for worldview integration.

The various types of integration mentioned in chapter three are:

1. *Subject-to-subject* integration: sometimes called multidisciplinary, interdisciplinary, or thematic integration.

2. *Subject-to-life* integration: sometimes referred to as authentic learning.

3. *Subject-to-worldview* integration: using biblical answers to life's biggest questions as the integrating core.

Subject-to-subject and subject-to-life integration can be done using activities found in curricular materials (such as the suggested research into the Cardiff Giant and Piltdown Man). This opens opportunities for subject-to-worldview learning.

Note for teachers of young children:

What children already believe to be true and the limits of their vocabulary and previous experiences must be considered. We *cannot* assume that they have biblical truths stored in their mind. We *can* assume, however, that they have misconceptions or incomplete knowledge as we all do.

Examples of Student Processing Activities

Curriculum Materials in Elementary Grades

This example was referenced in chapter seven. I was substituting for a second grade teacher, and one of the stories in the second grade reader was about a Native American boy who had been born sickly. The teacher's edition encourages the classroom teacher to highlight the last line of the story: *Isn't it wonderful that we have the gift of language to talk to ourselves in time of need?* This question triggered a connection: yes, the gift of language is wonderful. It also triggered a distinction: we have someone higher than ourselves to whom we can talk (parents and God who designed the family, etc).

The suggestion in the text spurred subject-to-subject integration: we discussed how human language and the ability to communicate are gifts from God, and exist because humans are created in the image of God. Discussing what we might have done to help the little boy, and applying that to a classmate who had been ill, was subject-to-life integration.

This is an illustration of looking for opportunities and having a disposition to do worldview integration. The story addresses several worldview questions: What is a human being? A communicator by nature. Is there someone higher than we are to talk to in times of need? There is a God who loves and cares for us and he uses parents and caretakers to care for us too. What kind of person does God want us to be? Compassionate and loving because when we are, we are more like Him and reflect His character. We show love and compassion when we send "get well" notes to those who are sick and to tell them that we are praying for them.

Continued Study in Middle School

In my fifth year of teaching, I started a program for gifted children in the Christian school in which I worked. One day in the course of discussion, one of my gifted students asked, "This book says dinosaurs died out 70 million years before man walked on this planet. The Bible says that on the sixth day of creation all beasts and creeping things *and* man were created. How do you explain that?"

This question caused some disequilibrium—for me!

I did not have an answer. I had some basic notions about the views and interpretations of the first several chapters of Genesis. Up to that time, I had done little research on dinosaurs. The question sparked a month of continued discussion.

During the ensuing research, one student wondered whether or not a dinosaur or two could have fit on Noah's ark. We measured a section of the school parking lot to determine the size of the ark. We compared it with the Nina, Pinta, and Santa Maria. Two of the gifted students, after calculating the volume of the ark, determined that two dinosaurs could fit with room to spare.

We compared the ratio of the ark to the accepted ideal ratio of seafaring ships today. A former Philadelphia shipyard worker visited the class and shared that the ships built today use the ratio God built into the dimensions of the ark. My kids were surprised that the ark was built with an effective ratio to prevent sinking. One of the boys in the gifted program built a replica of the ark to scale for his science project. He submitted it to hydraulic and wind testing to try to sink it.

This is worldview integration! It led to correlative activities that answered the questions, "What is ultimate reality?" (God); "What kind of God is He?" (He is smart! He is a creative designer!); "What is a human being?" (One who, created in the image of God, can think mathematically and spatially, build, and use knowledge and skills).

All this started because I led my students in research about a subject I didn't know well. Some years ago, orthodox Jews in Jerusalem threatened to boycott a milk company for putting pictures of dinosaurs on cartons of milk. One Jewish man admitted that when he purchased an encyclopedia, he cut out all of the parts that did not fit with his religion. That isn't intellectual coherence—it's intellectual suicide! If dinosaurs existed (and they did), they are God's creation and need to be studied in light of His perspective! I wanted my students to appreciate the fact that dinosaurs were created by God. They can be assured of that in spite of the fact that some of our conclusions were tentative in nature. This is an example of continued study that arises out of a cognitive interactive lesson plan. I had not planned to study dinosaurs in depth and certainly had not planned to study the measurements of the ark. These activities were promoted by the students.

Connection and Distinction in Senior Year

In a twelfth grade science book, I found the following illustration.

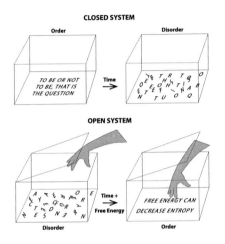

The illustration is meant to explain how order can come out of disorder; the textbook proposes that, just as we use energy to put together a puzzle that wouldn't otherwise fall in place, the sun's free energy helped "organize" evolution on the earth's surface. The text also calls attention to the "mysterious hand," noting that the analogy is not exact because "it implies the energy is somehow directed." Finally, the text claims that most theologians would think the energy is directed by God, but not many scientists would agree.

This curriculum component launched an interesting correlative/connective activity designed to explore why some direction by an outside force—God—was necessary to explain life as we understand it today; even the textbook editors sensed the need to provide a "hand in the box."

These questions can be used to create activities for students:

1) *Why do you think the editors of this text say that not many scientists call the director God?*

Have students find organizations for scientists who are Christians. They contact at least one member and ask the scientists to respond to the idea that not many scientists see a need for God. This research assignment is designed to show that there are indeed scientists (perhaps many scientists) who believe that the "director" is God. Today, I might have students research someone like Francis Collins, an American physician and geneticist, leader in the Human Genome Project, director of the National Institutes of Health, and author of *The Language of God: A Scientist Presents Evidence for Belief.*

2) *Why do you think it was necessary for the author and illustrator to use the analogy of a hand?*

Students are directed to research information theory and/or the concept of intelligent design in scientific journals, draw conclusions from their research concerning the "hand in the box," and be ready for a class discussion. This research assignment will yield varied results. Some students will seriously study intelligent design or information theory; others will just very quickly come up with one or two ideas; still others will encounter the writings of atheistic naturalists, who conclude that humans are simply very lucky to exist on a life-sustaining planet despite the absence of a designer. Teachers should be prepared to provide references and resources for the students. This is a *connection* activity designed to demonstrate that even non-Christian scientists and science editors feel compelled to see in nature the appearance of design and to find ways to illustrate that concept.

These two activities are integral to the introduction of the mini-unit. The suggestions come right out of the secular textbook.

3) *Why did the authors of the text think that theologians might call the director God? What do you think?*

Have the students define theology and then answer the question above. Then instruct them to find at least one Scripture passage theologians might use as evidence for their belief that God is the director of order in the universe.

In answering the first question, students integrate their findings, use additional research to make a judgment, and draw a conclusion based upon information obtained.

In the second question, students are provided an opportunity for speculation based upon current and new knowledge and worldview answers. Activities also encourage further reading and research of either information theory or intelligent design theory. One of the characteristics of effective critical thinking is to verify answers by continuing to read and research.

In the third question, the student is provided an opportunity to enhance a growing biblical worldview that acknowledges that those who spend a lifetime studying God and His Word find ample reasons to acknowledge and give God credit for His creation and sustaining work in the universe. Students will find out a little about theologians, their life work, and find evidence for their intelligent conclusions about God as "director."

The following can function as a final assessment:

> A Christian friend of yours, who is planning to study the natural sciences in college next year, tells you that what you are learning about God and the natural world is unacceptable to those pursuing a career in science. Write a response to your friend's comment using what you have concluded from the three worldview research assignments for this unit. Be thorough.

Full Unit Activity

Several high school literatures courses read *The Scarlet Letter*, a classic American novel by Nathaniel Hawthorne. A former student of mine, while teaching the novel, had her students chart the three worldviews addressed in the novel using a template provided in Leland Ryken's book, *Culture and Christian Perspective*.

Character	Puritans	Hester Prynne	Reverend Dimmesdale
Worldview	Legalism	Romanticism	Christian Theism
Central Theme	The moral code; Condemnation of violators	Feelings and human freedom; individual vs. society	God and His will; obedience, forgiveness and restoration
Quotes	"At the very least, they should have put the brand of a hot iron on Hester Prynne's forehead. Madame Hester would have winced at that, I warrant me. But she, —the naughty baggage, — little will she care what they put upon the bodice of her gown!"	"What we did had a consecration of its own ... we felt it so!"	"God's eye beheld it." "We forgot our God."

Afterward, students were to read the story of Joseph and Potiphar's wife in Genesis 39 and compare the events of the two stories to worldview issues in as many ways as they could. This was both connective and distinctive. Students were asked to record in their journals the worldview that was closest to their own views and why. Later, they used this journal entry for an assessment activity. These continuing activities are important; the chart alone would not have required *critical thinking* and therefore would not have led to worldview integration.

I sat in on the final day of this unit and was amazed at the students' responses. The students themselves discussed the behavior of a Christian on dates and in homes when no one was around. They spoke frankly, and yet were open to allowing God's perspective to speak to the issue of how we know right and wrong regarding premarital sex and adultery. One student pointed out that Joseph, although in a foreign land, did not "forget his God," the sin which Reverend Dimmesdale lamented. Another student argued that this only got Joseph in jail, and yet another student replied, "But God was with him in jail and used this to eventually get him to the place of second administrator in the country." All this occurred with very little teacher prompting.

There was no teacher devotional and no student boredom. Scripture spoke. Although there is no assurance that any minds and lives were changed, these students now had some stored biblical information that God's Spirit could bring to mind in a moment of temptation, and it was made more real through an integrated literature unit.

This is biblical worldview integration.

ACTIVITY

Examine your lesson plans to identify *student processing activities*. How might these be adapted to connect or distinguish a biblical worldview and the worldview addressed in the lesson or unit? Appendix Three contains an example Bible lesson using this model.

Fifteen

A Planning Cycle for Worldview Integration

"Where do I begin?"

I love to hear this question because it indicates that standing before me is one who really wants to teach worldview thinking in the school curriculum. Sometimes, however, an administrator will follow my presentation with the mandate for teachers to make sure that biblical integration is done in every lesson. I know that the administrator means well and really wants a school that promotes worldview integration, but I also know that the approach in this book is limited to the places in the curriculum where worldview questions are identified in the lesson and where activities to process the lesson information can be done naturally rather than tacked on. This chapter is dedicated to the task of helping teachers get started with the task of worldview integration.

After understanding worldview thinking and a worldview approach to biblical integration in the curriculum, one might use the following *planning* cycle.

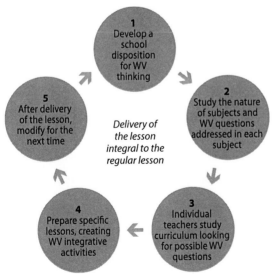

At number four in the cycle, individual teachers are planning individual lessons or units. Below is a way to think about lesson planning that helps a teacher avoid just tacking on something biblical to the lesson rather than embedding it naturally into the lesson. Start with a lesson plan template. I have used the cognitive interactive plan described in Chapter 13.

Developing a Regular Cognitive Interactive Lesson Plan

Study and Preparation

1. Study the materials and determine the *big idea* of the lesson. Highlight the relevant events, concepts, facts, ideas, or skill development sequence to expand and reinforce the big idea.

2. Formulate a target understanding and response and convert these targets into instructional objective(s). ("The student will be able to...")

3. Ask: "How will I know whether or not the student understands and can use the new learning?" Refer to the big idea. Write a tentative assessment activity in the plan: a scenario, performance, or question.

4. Ask: "What worldview questions are addressed and answered in this lesson?" If one is identified, write it, answer it, and be ready to develop an objective, a possible assessment, and an activity.

Recall the four elements of a cognitive interactive lesson plan:

- Motivation
- New information/concept or skill development
- Student processing activities
- Assessment

Delivery

5. Design a motivation activity to engage the mind. When possible, use the prior knowledge and experiences of the student or arouse curiosity or set up a question or problem. Make sure this activity fits with the big idea of the lesson in some way and is not designed just to get attention. The motivation activity may also be an introduction to the worldview processing activity in the lesson.

6. Provide a way for the student to receive the new information: labs, hands-on activities, guided inductive study, writing and sharing, discovery of a rule, research activity, storytelling, lecture, DVD or video, Internet search, paraphrased reading/writing response to content, etc.

7. Design student processing activities to help promote understanding and/or envision action. Ask: "How can the students fit in the new information with previous knowledge and their own life experience and developing biblical worldview?" This part of the

lesson is essential for worldview integration.

8. Revise or add the tentative assessment. Worldview learning should be assessed as part of the lesson, just as any other school learning. For the summative assessment for a mini-unit, the worldview integration assessment should be assessed alongside the unit; it should not be assessed separately.

Expanding Worldview Integrative Planning

1. Take a lesson you have studied and laid out on the plan above or some other plan you use. Develop the lesson with a big idea, important related facts, and student processing activities. I recommend using the cognitive interactive model if you have no other preference.

2. If you identified any worldview questions in the lesson material, do the following:

   a) Write and answer the worldview question(s). This is important for keeping focused.

   b) State the general worldview question and write it specifically for the lesson at hand. If, for example, you are studying seeds in plants and the cycle of growth, the broad worldview question is, "What is the nature of the external world?" A sub-question specific to this lesson is, "How did God design the world of plant life in order to sustain living things?" A lesson on seeded plants and the food cycle provides an opportunity to *connect* clearly to the worldview issue of God's sustaining work through the processes of nature, specifically seed-bearing plants (Genesis 1:29–30).

   c) Write a biblical worldview objective that fits the question(s) addressed and a tentative assessment. For the lesson on seeded plants, an example objective would be, "The student will be able to describe the cycle of growth for seeded plants and write a psalm of thanks to God for His design for food."

   As an assessment, teachers can use the pattern of a psalm, such as Psalm 136a: "Give thanks to the Lord, for …" Have the students finish the sentence using as much as they remember about their lesson on plants. The class can make a booklet of completed "psalms." (Use a rubric to help the students remember elements of the science unit or lesson).

3. In the lesson plan, find an appropriate place to insert a worldview activity—not a preaching message, but something the students do to connect or distinguish. Write the *student processing activity*.

a) Ask: "What can I have the students do to *connect* the content of the lesson with a biblical view of that question?" Write an activity or two. (Notice the importance: *student activity* promotes thinking better than a short devotional comment or two.)

b) Ask: "Is there anything in the lesson that must be *distinguished* from a biblical view because it is in clear conflict with God's perspective ?" If so, write a distinguishing activity.

Assessment is the final element of both the cognitive interactive teaching model and the worldview model suggested in this book. Both the instructional objective and the worldview objective should be assessed, ideally at the same time so that the biblical integration is seen as a regular and important part of the lesson.

The next chapter contains an example lesson on photosynthesis illustrated at various levels.

The Ultimate Assessment

There are several ways to describe when worldview integration is occurring.

1. When students begin to think biblically *on their own*, by taking note of materials in their curriculum that connect or are distinct from a biblical worldview. Even young children can hear or read something and declare, "This is like the person in the Bible who helped the Samaritan." Or, "The boy in this story might not be a Christian because he doesn't seem to thank God for creation." Older students will often bring in articles in which they have found things that relate to one of the big questions of life. I experience this frequently as a college teacher.

2. When the students' worldview related to a subject area aligns with God's point of view.

3. When students internalize God's special revelation about the world and life rather than dividing life and learning into secular and sacred parts.

4. When students are functioning, integrated people who view life holistically (rather than segmenting secular and sacred) and act and think in accordance with a biblical belief core. Worldviews may seem integrated in the classroom but be abandoned on the basketball court.

5. When students view all of life and learning from God's perspective, not from "under the sun." The teacher in Ecclesiastes pursued academics (study and exploration), pleasure,

work (career), achievement, projects, and riches—and found them all meaningless "under the sun" (without God).

6. When biblical answers to life's biggest questions become the "glue" that holds the curriculum together as a coherent whole and students develop intellectual coherency around biblical truth claims evidenced in their thinking and acting.

The only way to develop the skill of worldview integration is to do what you understand at the moment and ask God for wisdom in understanding and integrating His Word. It takes much more than desire to accomplish this task. It takes study, planning, and hard work. But it is eternally worth it!

Worldview Integration and Specific Subject Areas

Certain subject areas lend themselves more easily to daily worldview integration; others are more effectively integrated by the unit rather than by individual lessons. Take science as an example. I have found that worldview integration can be done as part of a unit, but certainly not in lessons every day. By contrast, in elementary reading instruction, integrative activities might be done daily. As illustrated in the high school literature lesson for *The Scarlet Letter* in the previous chapter, integrative activities might be completed throughout the unit and then culminated at the end of the novel. In mathematics, the opportunity for integration using the conventional use of number and mathematical relationships is available at the elementary level more readily than at higher levels, where relationships and patterns are more abstract. Nevertheless, worldview thinking should be planned and included in mathematics classes. Galileo wrote, "Mathematics is the language with which God has written the universe." Math can answer worldview questions about ultimate reality, the nature of the external world, and the nature of human beings.

- God exists and has created a world of precision that allows patterns and relationships to be consistent and predictable.

- God created the cosmos with its inherent number and spatial patterns and relationships. Mathematics is in the mind of God and used in creation and invention. (Disney's *Donald Duck in Mathmagic Land* is an excellent resource for communicating this idea.)

- Humans, created in the image of God, have the capacity to think about and communicate God's mathematical concepts and ideas.

- The visible and invisible speak of God's power, design, and sustaining work. His wisdom and glory are evident in nature and mathematics.

- God communicates quantitatively and reveals His relationships and patterns in such a way that humans, created in the image of God, can create systems, construct relationships, and think about reality.

ACTIVITY

Take the eight worldview questions and try to determine additional sub-issues and questions in your own area of teaching. Then add other areas that you will use for subject-to-subject integration. In Appendix Three, I have included the work of one of my university undergraduate classes completing this activity in class.

Sixteen

Example of a Worldview Approach to Biblical Integration

Examples can be helpful in seeing how to flesh out a model. A sample of teaching a Bible lesson using a cognitive interactive approach is provided in Appendix Three. Additional examples are found in previous chapters. This chapter provides a more extensive example on a single, widely taught topic.

A schoolwide worldview approach to biblical integration can help combat the inability to articulate one's worldview, a problem experienced by many Christians. This approach can also help prevent the absorption of the prevailing views in the culture. However, if a school does not practice biblical worldview integration, individual teachers can still determine to do the best they can with the students God has given them.

A Non-Example of Biblical Integration

Sometimes it is helpful to envision what biblical integration *is not* in order to solidify *what it is*. In a workshop for school administrators on the topic of biblical integration, delegates were asked to share some of the ways their teachers were carrying out the mandate for biblical integration in their schools.

One administrator said, "For a lesson on photosynthesis, a sixth grade teacher had the students compare the elements plants need to make food to what we need in our spiritual lives to grow." The teacher's PowerPoint looked something like this:

Sun — Son (the Son of God)

Water — Word (the Word of God)

Air — Spirit (the Holy Spirit)

There is nothing wrong with using analogies to describe spiritual concepts. Jesus compared Himself to bread, light, a good shepherd, and so on. Clearly, however, this is not a worldview approach to biblical integration. It takes the mind of the student away from the lesson at hand and moves it to spiritual growth; it becomes a devotional substitute for the connecting or distinguishing biblical answers to the worldview issue of the nature of the external world; and it *substitutes* Bible teaching for integrated science teaching and thus further develops a dichotomy of thinking. It may even contribute to the practice of separating the "secular" from the "sacred."

True Biblical Integration

The example below uses the integrating core model developed in this book to integrate photosynthesis with a biblical worldview. Activities are first developed for lower elementary and then for middle school or early high school.

Concept: Photosynthesis

Preparing the Lesson

1) The teacher will thoroughly prepare the individual science lessons or unit. I recommend the use of the cognitive interactive model/template described in this book. It fits very well with a directed inquiry approach to science. Having a disposition toward a worldview approach to biblical integration, the teacher will study the unit and proposed lessons looking for worldview questions addressed. Since this is a science unit, it will at least address the nature of the external world.

2) In understanding the structure of science and the worldview issues usually addressed, the teacher might list the broadly stated worldview issues in science: God exists; God designed and created; God sustains His creation using laws He has built into nature and using humans He created with the capacity to discover and use those laws (part of the cultural mandate); His creatures owe Him thanks. (Romans 11:36 and Acts 17 are good passages to remind us of the last one).

3) Worldview questions addressed in the lesson or mini-unit are numerous. The teacher writes these and answers them. For example:

What is the nature of the external world? (Designed, created.) The teacher determines whether or not this concept is evident, tacitly omitted, or challenged in the lesson.

What kind of God is the Creator? (Loving sustainer.) Is the concept of sustaining life as a result of the process of photosynthesis evident in the lesson?

What is a human being? (One who is created to discover and learn about God's laws of nature, to use them for good, and to be thankful for what God has created and His ongoing provisions for life.) How are humans portrayed in the lesson, especially in the relationships among plants, animals, and humans?

4) A teacher might think, "My desire as a science teacher is to teach the subject with excellence. Biblical integration does not substitute a Bible lesson for the science lesson. It teaches good science, brings the new knowledge together with issues, and answers worldview questions from a biblical perspective that give meaning to the Christian life. The science knowledge is vital, a part of God's revelation to humans."

In addition, a teacher who is thinking biblically with a disposition toward worldview integration might think, "My desire as a *Christian teacher* is to consciously connect the new science learning to the God who provides our food and oxygen through that process and thus sustains our lives. We owe Him thanks for our continued existence— for life itself!"

5) Once the worldview questions have been specified and written in terms specific to the lesson or unit, an objective will be written that *includes* a worldview issue or a worldview objective will be written separately. Below are several worldview objectives that might we used when photosynthesis is taught in the early elementary and middle school levels.

EARLY ELEMENTARY UNIT

Big idea objective of the mini-unit: Photosynthesis is one of the most important natural processes on our planet.

Unit objective: The student will be able to describe the relationship among humans, animals, and plants in the process of photosynthesis.

Lesson objective: The student will be able to define "photosynthesis" and identify the elements that are needed for photosynthesis to occur.

Worldview objective: Using the definition of photosynthesis and the elements required in order for plants to make food, the student will be able to articulate why we owe thanks to God for our food.

Later in the unit, a lesson will be taught on what humans contribute to the process (the carbon dioxide that we breathe out) and what plants contribute to our environment (the oxygen for humans to breathe in).

MIDDLE SCHOOL UNIT

Unit objective: The student will be able to construct a scientific explanation for the role of photosynthesis in the cycling of matter and flow of energy into and out of organisms. (Plants make their own food. Food for animals and for humans comes from both plants and animals that eat plants.)

Worldview objective: The student will be able to use a scientific explanation to show how living things (humans, animals, and plants) depend upon plant life for food by connecting the water cycle (H_2O), the gas cycle (O and CO_2), and the energy source (the sun). The student will be able to *defend* why we owe God thanks for "life."

Note the difference between the lower level and middle school. One tells why we owe God thanks for our food, a very concrete concept. The other is broader and a bit deeper: the students must defend why we owe God thanks for life itself.

6) Using the objective, the teacher would consider a tentative assessment to come back to after the complete planning of the worldview activities.

Process for lower elementary teacher: What connection is there between the elements of the process and a biblical view of the elements? Certainly the elements are mentioned in Scripture and attributed to the God of Creation. What is the response that humans should have to these created elements and this life saving and sustaining process? The question in the text is answered by telling kids how important it is to care for plant life because we get food and oxygen from plants. This is a great *connection* but the text does not give the Creator of the process any credit. Rather, the credit goes to the continued natural processes and by inference, Nature (usually in caps), "which is to be revered." This latter comment is found in curriculum materials at a growing rate and is indicative of naturalistic pantheism.

The teacher might create an activity to identify in the Bible the ultimate source of the elements needed for the process and the connection to food, or develop an activity to connect God not only to the elements needed, but to the process and product that sustains human life. Use questions like, "Why do we pray before we eat here at school?" "Why do some people call praying 'saying grace'?" "What is grace?"

Now the teacher has some guidance to help in planning activities and assessment. The assessment is connected to the objective; the objective is worked out through the lesson plan activities, and then assessed.

Process for the middle school teacher: What connection is there between the cycle of oxygen and carbon dioxide, the energy of the sun, water, and chlorophyll? How might that connection be an example of intelligence and design in creation? This thinking will assist in envisioning how the students might be assessed.

Example Worldview Integrative Activities

This is not a complete lesson/unit plan, but rather an example of the integrative activities in the *student processing activities* part of an interactive lesson. Both lower- and upper-level activities are provided here as examples only.

Subject Area: Science, Lower Elementary Level

Unit: Photosynthesis—the food-making process in plants. The text states this is the most important natural process on our planet.

Unit big idea: All life (human, animal, and plant) depends on this process to survive.

Sub-ideas:

- Photosynthesis is the process plants use to make their own food and food for animals and humans.
- The leaves of the plants contain chlorophyll that absorbs the energy from the sun.
- Chlorophyll, water, carbon dioxide, and the energy of the sun make photosynthesis possible.

Background information:

- Plants capture light energy (the sun) and use that energy to make sugar (food).
- The chlorophyll in the plant absorbs the sunlight.
- The sunlight is combined with water and carbon dioxide.
- The plant leaves process the ingredients and make sugar (food) and oxygen.
- Plants give us food and the air we breathe.

The process takes air that humans and animals breathe out, water, and the energy of sunlight to make food in the chloroplast of the plant. In the process, plants give us the air we need to breathe. Plants and animals need each other to survive.

The text says, "Animals including humans make the CO_2 (carbon dioxide) plants need. They (the plants) make the O_2 (oxygen) and food we need."

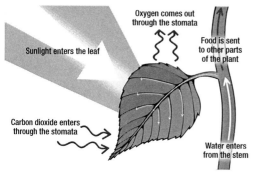

Oxygen comes out through the stomata

Sunlight enters the leaf

Food is sent to other parts of the plant

Carbon dioxide enters through the stomata

Water enters from the stem

There is much to connect to the God who made the plants, designed the interchange of oxygen and carbon dioxide, created the sun and water cycle, and has given humankind the task of caring for His created world. What might be distinguished in the lesson material? The text I was using at the time classified humans as animals. This is not a biblically ordered classification. This would be a place to use the early chapters of Genesis, which state humans, and humans alone, are created in the image and likeness of God (Genesis 9:6).

Engaging lesson: Teach the science lesson and plan to use a processing activity or two for biblical worldview integration, perhaps beginning in the *motivation element* of the lesson if appropriate.

Student motivating activity: Hand out paper plates and have the students draw their favorite foods.

Ask: Where does the food on your plates come from? Pair share and then share together as a class. Some answers might be: "the store," "the farmer and his crops," "mom or dad," or "plants and animals."

Bridge: What if there were no planted crops, no farmers, no stores, and nothing to bring home? What would happen? Tell your partner. (We might die and certainly we would be hungry.) I am glad we have all of these things. Today, we are going to find out where our food really comes from and a very special way God designed it so that we can have food to eat.

As a part of the motivation, the teacher might wish to tell the story from Exodus 16 of God providing manna in the wilderness for the Israelites. Begin the story with the earlier hypothetical: "What if there were no planted crops, no farmers, no stores, and nothing to bring home? Well, this really happened to a group of people in the Bible who had lived for a long time in Egypt and were now moving to a land that God had given to them. The trip was long and soon they ran out of food.... Listen to find out what *very special thing* God did for them to provide food."

Then the teacher tells the story and emphasizes that God does not send manna on the ground for us anymore, but He does use a *very special process that He created.* Let's find out about that special process in our science lesson today. How does God provide food for us now?

Further methods for lesson: Hands-on activities, storytelling, YouTube clips of the process, pictures and tell, etc.

A key concept in the lesson at this level is the list of the essential elements needed to produce food and oxygen. Plants need the right ingredients to produce the food they need and we need. The definition of photosynthesis tells us that sunlight (*photo*) is needed for energy and that energy "puts together" (*synthesis*) the elements to make the food.

Worldview processing activities:

Provide a chart like this one for each student. I recommend using light green paper, if possible.

Ask the students to draw the three elements needed by the plant to make food (air, sun, and rain). Below is one example.

Air is often drawn as a puffy cloud (though I did have one student who drew a pair of jeans hanging on a clothesline and blowing in the wind). Water is usually depicted as drops, and the sun is usually a circle colored yellow. But as long as the pictures depict the element, the student's drawings are accepted.

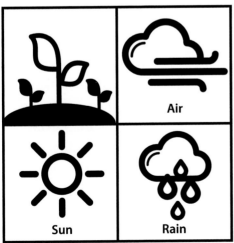

Then, in pairs, the students are to look at the verses on the handout and connect food with any element needed for food-making in plants.

"As the *rain and the snow* come down from heaven, and do not return to it without watering the earth and *making it bud and flourish,* so that it yields seed for the sower and *bread* for the eater." —Isaiah 55:10

Draw a conclusion about the relationship between water and food and explain your thinking using your science lesson. With very early elementary, you might have them finish a sentence: "One very important element in the special way God provides our food is...." "How do we know that water is so important to food?"

In the verse below, have students color the words for water in green and words for food in red and draw a conclusion. What can we say about rain and food? Why should we thank God for food?

> You care for the land and water it; you enrich it abundantly. The streams of God are filled with water to provide the people with grain, for so you have ordained it. You drench its furrows and level its ridges; you soften it with showers and bless its crops. You crown the year with your bounty, and your carts overflow with abundance.

> —Psalm 65:9–11

Ask: "What element in the process of photosynthesis is connected to food in this verse? To whom should we give thanks for food and for the process that makes food and why? Tell your neighbor. Find the part of the verse that you used to tell why and read it to the class. Who is the 'you' referring to in 'you enriched it abundantly?'" Check out the vocabulary words that can be taught though this activity: enrich, drench, furrows, ridges, bounty, abundance, ordained.

Have students complete the chart below using the provided Scripture references. Their work is illustrated in italics.

Element and products	Scripture Reference	Summary Idea
Sun	Genesis 1:16 Psalm 136:7-9	*God created "lights"* *Sun and moon*
Rain	Matthew 5:45 Job 36:27-31	*Sun and rain, God's gifts for all (as* *common grace)*
Air	Acts 17:25	*Breath and life from God*
Food	Psalm 65:9-11 Isaiah 55:10	*Food we eat is a gift of God as He uses the* *process and the elements He created*

Further directions: Using the chart and the verses on your handout (Isaiah 55:11; Psalm 65:9–11), write a sentence that tells why we should thank God for our food.

Do not have kids simply look up verses without connecting questions or drawing conclusions. The purpose here is to connect these created and life-sustaining elements of photosynthesis to food and God's provision for life. Sun, air, and rain must be connected to food and life. The last verses in the chart show a connection and enhance what we are learning about photosynthesis.

Activity: Write a class song using the elements needed for photosynthesis. I did this with the praise chorus, *God Is So Good*. Each verse after the first is suggested by a student and repeated.

God is so good,	*He gives us food;*	*He sends the rain...* (v. three)
God is so good,	*He gives us food;*	*He made the sun...* (v. four)
God is so good,	*He gives us food;*	*He gives us air...* (v. five)
He's so good to me	*He's so good to me.*	*He is so good to me!*

Then add this song to the class song book to help remind us to thank God for the food that He provides through His very special plan of photosynthesis! Print the song and use it as a reminder before lunch on several days. Add it to your binder of class-created songs.

Alternate activity: Take a picture of the class praying for food at lunch time. Project the picture and ask the students to use what they learned in their science lesson to tell why it is a good idea to pray before we eat. Why do we thank God for our food? Why did farmers stop to thank God for food at harvest time in early America? (Connect it to history and abundance and bounty.) Why do you think we have "Thanksgiving?"

Psalm 136:25–26a: "He gives food to every creature. His love endures forever. Give thanks to the God of heaven." Scan copies of the class picture and place the verse under the picture.

Assessment: "Pretend that a new friend at school does not understand why we give thanks to God before we eat our lunch. Explain to him how the food we eat is related to God our Creator and why we owe Him thanks. Use your science knowledge of God's special design for food-making in plants; use God's provision for the children of Israel in the wilderness, and the Bible verse we wrote under our picture. The new boy really loves history and science."

This can be a pair-share activity where the students take turns being the new student or a written assignment, depending on grade level.

SUBJECT AREA: SCIENCE, MIDDLE SCHOOL LEVEL

Unit big idea: All life (human and animal) depends upon plant life for food. Plants make their food using the provisions found in the creative order provided by the Creator (water, carbon dioxide, chlorophyll, and the energy of the sun), and the process He designed and sustains. Plants not only provide food but also oxygen. Animals and humans provide carbon dioxide for the process.

Unit objective: The student will be able to construct a scientific explanation for the role of photosynthesis in the cycling of matter and flow of energy into and out of organisms. (Plants make their own food. Food for animals and for humans comes from both plants and animals that eat plants.)

Worldview objective: The student will be able to use a scientific explanation to show how living things (humans, animals, and plants) depend upon plant life for food by connecting the water cycle (H_2O), the gas cycle (O_2 and CO_2), and the energy source (the sun). The student will be able to *defend* why we owe God thanks for "life."

Unit background: The process of photosynthesis is a *chemical reaction*. Scientists believe that it is the most important chemical reaction on our planet.

Photosynthesis is the process whereby plants use the light energy from the sun to convert carbon dioxide and water to glucose and oxygen through a series of reactions. The overall equation for photosynthesis is carbon dioxide + water + light energy → glucose + oxygen.

$$6CO_2 + 6H_2O \quad \xrightarrow[\text{chlorophyll}]{\text{light energy}} \quad C_6H_{12}O_6 + 6O_2$$

The unit includes a review of the water cycle and the gas cycle (oxygen and carbon dioxide) and a study of the source of energy for the process. It includes the basic chemical reaction that takes place in the factory of the leaf using the required elements.

Interactive lesson activities: At the middle grade level, students will set up experiments to test the need for each element. Labs for this activity suggest a control plant. The control plant has access to all of the elements: water, sunlight, and plenty of air. A second plant receives water and air, but no light (and is accordingly labeled); a third receives light and air but no water; the last receives water and light but is cut off from air as much as possible. Pictures are taken, dated, and posted at two- to three-day intervals for the extent of the unit. Leaves are tested by the students for the presence of glucose (using iodine) at the beginning and the end.

Unit skills:

- Experimentation
- Use of a control plant and experimental plants
- Operational definitions

- Hypothesis making and testing
- Drawing conclusions and predicting
- Using conclusions—"science in society" (authentic situation)

Textbook material: The text says, "All animal life, including humans, owes its survival to this process; plant life depends on carbon dioxide that animals breathe out. We revere the processes of nature as they sustain life on this planet."

Photosynthesis produces glucose and oxygen. Both of these are required by humans for respiration, which is how humans make the energy required to perform all cellular activities. Without access to the products of photosynthesis, the human race would cease to exist.

In the process of changing light energy to chemical energy in photosynthesis, the sun is the ultimate source of energy.

- Plants need light energy, CO_2, and H_2O
- The process occurs in plants and some algae
- Energy is stored as sugar
- The process takes place in the chloroplasts using chlorophyll

This chart could also be used at the middle school level with additional directions added to those described above for lower elementary.

Element and products	Scripture Reference	Summary Idea
Sun	Genesis 1:16	*Created "lights"*
	Psalm 136:7–9	*Sun and moon*
Rain	Matthew 5:45	*Sun and rain for all*
	Job 36:27–31	*(as common grace)*
Air	Acts 17:25	*Breath and life*
Food	Psalm 65:9–11	*Food we eat*
	Isaiah 55:10	

Unit lesson: One of the lessons uses red, blue, and green blocks to represent carbon, oxygen, and hydrogen. Students use the blocks to develop the equation for glucose. It is a carbohydrate, a type of sugar. *6CO$_2$ + 6H$_2$O + light energy > C$_6$H$_{12}$O$_6$ + 6O$_2$*

Plants collect water through their roots; water is made up of molecules. A water molecule is made with the elements of hydrogen and oxygen. In each molecule of water there are two hydrogen atoms and one oxygen atom. Many students will know this and call water H_2O.

Carbon dioxide is also needed for photosynthesis. The air is made up of several gases. Carbon dioxide is one of them. In fact when we breathe in, we take in oxygen and when we breathe out we give out carbon dioxide. It is also a molecule, with the formula CO_2. Some students will know this as well. How many atoms of carbon and oxygen are there in CO_2? One atom of carbon and two atoms of oxygen.

Student processing activities:

- *Connecting Activity:*

    The teacher might wonder, "What do I know from this unit about the design and nature of the process, the sustaining energy of the sun, the water source, and the exchange of gasses in the air (especially CO_2 for plants provided by humans and the oxygen provided for us by plants) that would lead one to conclude that this process is one that God uses to sustain life?"

    Student Processing Activity: "Prepare a defense of the following statement: 'Scientists and Bible scholars believe that the process of photosynthesis is probably the most important natural process on planet earth.' You might begin this way, 'Scientists believe that the process of photosynthesis is the most important chemical reaction on the planet earth because ...' Be thorough and use the rubric to prepare your defense. Then: Bible teachers also believe that the process of photosynthesis is probably the most important process in nature because.... Use your unit on photosynthesis and at least two passages of Scripture that give God credit for one or more of the elements needed for plants to make food. Use any Bible helps you can find, hard copy or electronic."

The students would have had a brief history of the discovery of the process of photosynthesis and the conclusion, that while all of the elements needed for food-making in plants are mentioned and some are connected to food in God's Word, the process of photosynthesis was not discovered and named until the seventeenth and eighteenth centuries, and we are still discovering more about the chemical reaction today. Scientific investigation is part of the mandate that God gave to humans to subdue the earth and have dominion over it. Science is not at war with the Bible as some think. The underlying naturalistic philosophy of some scientists is the issue.

This is also a good place to help students understand that God has given humankind the capacity and mandate to have dominion over the living things on the earth, to discover patterns and relationships in nature, and to use these for the benefit of humankind as common grace and a reflection of God's glory (characteristics of humans that reflect God's character such as thought and creativity). Projects in third world countries designed to help people groups grow better crops might also be included as a part of "loving our neighbor." It is also a place to teach that while God's Word is indeed truth, not all truth is found in the Bible (such as the details about the chemical process in photosynthesis). It is also a place to help students understand that science knowledge is always open to change as humans continue to investigate and discover. Actually, this is true of what we know about photosynthesis and plant growth as well.

- *Distinguishing Activity*

The teacher might wonder, "What do I do when there is a clear contradiction between a biblical worldview answer and an answer provided by the text, film clip, etc. to one of the big questions of life?"

Have the students read the sentence in the text or put it on a PowerPoint slide. The text says, "The sun is the *ultimate* source of energy for the process of photosynthesis." This is true scientifically; the sun is the energy source. In my class, I challenged the word "ultimate."

Ask the students to define "ultimate." Discuss their definitions. Can you think of any reasons for calling the sun the ultimate source of energy? (Its light is essential for the chemical reaction.) Can you think of any reason for not calling the sun the *ultimate* source of energy based upon the definition of the word ultimate? (Who created the sun?)

The God who made the sun is the *ultimate* source of energy and Creator of all things. This is not just a technicality or trying to deal with a minuscule feature of the process and certainly not an attempt to take the mind of the students off the science itself. The belief that the sun is ultimate has led to sun worship throughout the centuries—it even exists today in naturalistic pantheism.

Processing activity: Design an activity to critique the idea that the sun is the *ultimate* source of energy. This can be done using subject-to-subject integration.

Social studies integration: For people in ancient Egypt, the sun was a source of life. It was power and energy, light and warmth. It was what made the crops grow each season, so it is no surprise that the cult of Ra had immense power. Ra was the ruler of the heavens. He was the god of the sun, the bringer of light, and patron to the pharaohs.

Have the students research Ra and suggest theories for why the Egyptians worshiped the sun.

Students will likely conclude that the Egyptians were intelligent: they knew the sun was the essential energy source for plants to grow food that sustains life, but they did not know the God who created the sun. So they worshipped what they thought was the ultimate provider of food and life.

Alternate processing activity: Have the students look up the passages in Deuteronomy 4:15–19 and Job 31:26–28 to find out what God forbade His people to do. Relate their findings to the social studies passage that tells about sun worship. (God warned the Israelites not to form any kind of idols to worship. Israel was forbidden to worship the sun, stars, and moon; the practice displeased God very much. These were the practices of nations that did not know the living God.)

"And when you look up to the sky and see the sun, the moon and the stars—all the heavenly array—do not be enticed into bowing down to them and worshiping things the Lord your God has apportioned to all the nations under heaven."

—Deuteronomy 4:19

God called "detestable" the practice of sun worship when Manasseh, king of Judah, was following the practices of the nations that did not know the Lord. Manasseh was worshipping the starry hosts (2 Kings 21:3).

In Ezekiel 8:16–17, when the Lord was showing His prophet the detestable things the Israelites were doing, He mentioned sun worship as especially detestable. They were charged with being worse than the nations around them.

"If I have regarded the sun in its radiance or the moon moving in splendor, so that my heart was secretly enticed and my hand offered them a kiss of homage, then these also would be sins to be judged, for I would have been unfaithful to God on high."

— Job 31:26–28

From the above seed ideas, could you design an activity for your grade level? Perhaps you might have the students read to find out the detestable practice of the Israelites and why God detested what they were doing (Ezekiel 11:12). God's people, who had a special relationship with Him, had conformed to the practices of the nations around them. But those nations did not know the Lord, so they worshipped what they knew provided food and life for them. It was not a matter of ignorance, but of not knowing the God of the universe. Even brilliant Greek philosophers were worshipping several gods and an unknown god—just in case they had missed one. The apostle Paul shared with them knowledge about "the God who made the world and everything in it ... He gives everyone life and *breath* and everything else" (Acts 17). Students need to understand that we look at science through the lens of Scripture, seeing the stars and sun and moon from God's perspective and giving Him thanks and praise. Others view the creation as an object of worship itself because they do not know the God of creation, but many do know the importance of the sun, water, and air.

Language arts integration: I used the Native American poem "New Moon" in conjunction with this lesson while teaching sixth graders.

New moon come out, give water to us

New moon thunder down, give water to us

New moon, shake down, give water to us

Hunger is bad

Hunger is like a lion

Hunger is bad

It makes us eat locusts

The Native Americans were not ignorant. They knew that the rain was vital to the growth of plants and they thought the moon had something to do with that growth. They knew plants sustained their lives and the lives of animals they used for clothing and food as well. So they reached out to the moon and worshipped it and they danced for rain. (This topic of the relationship between the moon and plant growth could be a continued study for someone in the class who might be interested. Is there any relationship? Research and find out what scientist have to say about this issue.)

Many people who rain-danced or worshipped the sun did so simply because they knew the importance of the sun and rain and air, the relationship among these elements, and the result—food and life. But they did not know the God who made the sun or sends the rain. Many intelligent people do not know God, including some scientists who are very intelligent but only know about the natural world.

Worldview thinking:

1. Do you see an opportunity here to discuss how we are to talk to people who hold unbiblical views, perhaps because they do not know God? We should never attack others by demeaning them, even when they do not hold the beliefs that we do. This is a practice too many participate in when looking at alternative worldviews that vie for our minds and heart. Youth need to know early in life that it is the ideas that may be different and may need to be defended. People should be respected.

2. God forbids the worship of the sun, the moon, or the stars for His people. Why might that be so? Have students read Romans 1:25a: "They exchanged the truth about God for a lie, and worshiped and served created things rather than the Creator." Write a sentence or two that clearly tells why a Christian does not worship the sun or rain even though we are thankful for both.

3. Do you see an opportunity here to create an activity to contrast astronomy and astrology for your upper-level students? Today's youth have instant access to horoscope information on the Internet, and many are caught up in the practice of consulting the stars daily.

Notice the integration of literature and social studies with science. Subject-to-subject integration is a very important aspect of worldview integration. It opens many doors. Worldview integration is the internalization of the connections between what is being studied and one's worldview.

Connections to a biblical worldview:

The concept of photosynthesis is connected to:

- Related facts and subjects (social studies and literature) and to the student's integrating core beliefs

- A biblical answer to the nature of the external world

- The exchange of gases in the air—appreciate and care for plants

- The water cycle—appreciate rain

- God's design to sustain life—thankful for the food on my plate

- Human stewardship

- Love for people who have other beliefs and worship nature rather than the God who created and sustains it

Possible worldview assessment: Write a psalm, poem, or song that begins, "Give thanks to the God of heaven who gives food to all."

Directions: "The poem must be at least three verses long and include the scientific details of the process of photosynthesis. Use the water cycle, the gas cycle, and the energy source in order to show your understanding of how these relate to the process of food-making in plants and reasons for giving thanks to God. Students might be asked to include in some way the chemical formula for the result of the process."

Provide a rubric that insures both scientific details and the connection to food and therefore to life.

Conclusion

My recommendation to those just beginning to develop a worldview approach to biblical integration is to look for opportunities and commit to trying to include at least one or two opportunities during the next several weeks. Do not force what is not there. Biblical worldview integration should flow naturally out of issues and questions. It should be an integral part of the regular lesson, not be seen by students as "the Christian part" that can be tolerated or just ignored. (Some students quickly learn that they will not be assessed on worldview learning except in Bible class.) This approach calls for assessment and evaluation integral to the curriculum. I have found that the more I think biblically, the more the skills for integrative teaching are strengthened.

Seventeen

Walking the Talk!

Worldview integration is more than a school mission or vision statement. It is more than a scurry of worldview activity before an accreditation team visit. It is more than a one-time professional development workshop. It is an ongoing intentional process that is carried out in the strategic design of the curriculum in a Christian academic institution.

Living a Biblical Worldview

A few years ago, I read *The Year of Living Biblically* by A. J. Jacobs, an agnostic Jew. It is a wonderful, hilarious, and provocative book recording a year-long project of living by the values and rules of the Bible as literally as possible. At the end of the year, Jacobs was still agnostic, but a more "reverent agnostic." He admitted that the process had made him more religious (though it was his own cafeteria religion) and a more thankful person. He wrote, "I'm not sure whom I'm thanking, but I have become addicted to the act of thanking."

A one-year long project! Some of us in Christian education will have our students for just one year; others will have many more. Biblical Christianity is more than trying to live the dos and don'ts of the Bible as external add-ons to life; it is more than Bible class or chapel (although these serve very important purposes in a Christian school). This book has offered an approach to the ongoing "project" of biblical worldview integration.

Recently in church, I sang along to "How Great is Our God." The song brought to mind a contrast to Christopher Hitchens' book, *God Is Not Great*, mentioned earlier in this book. It struck me that the world needs more than our singing—more than the call to "sing with me how great is our God." Our world needs to see Christians live wholly for God with undivided hearts and minds, viewing all of life from God's perspective—walking the talk.

Christianity is more than small group or Sunday morning worship. It is more than singing of the greatness of God, although music is such a natural way to praise the Lord and I love it! It is more than memorizing verses and praying. Rather, it is a change in thinking and acting in accordance with a biblically informed mind and it should penetrate all of life. It should lead to knowing the One we thank, and it should last beyond the years we may have the students. Our scholarship and academic activities should soundly manifest a distinctively Christian worldview. It takes not only a disposition and know-how, but also dedicated work. But it is eternally worth it!

We live at a time in history when sociologists have identified popular "Christianity" among our youth as something other than orthodox biblical Christianity. This popular version is not understood to be a particular worldview, but rather a new "religion" heavily influenced by the ideology of individualism. Researchers from the University of North Carolina have concluded that youth today have a set of beliefs that have been self-chosen (Smith and Lundquist Denton). This echoes the self-chosen beliefs shown in *Life of Pi*.

Some of the beliefs of this generation of youth include a belief in God. For example: There is a God who created the world and *is available when we have a problem*. The primary goal of life is to *be happy and to feel good about oneself*. God wants people to be nice and fair with each other as taught by most world religions. These beliefs have been categorized under the label "Moralistic Therapeutic Deism." "The radical transformation of Christian theology and Christian beliefs replaces the sovereignty of God with the sovereignty of self" (Mohler 2015).

If he were alive today, what would Abraham Kuyper say about the supreme sovereignty vying for the minds of youth in our generation? That sovereignty has moved from the church, to the state, to science, and now to the *self*! The human self has become the starting point of several very popular worldviews. This "Selfie" generation is the cultural context in which God has called us to teach the young.

Conclusion

Developing biblical worldview integration in the strategic design of the curriculum will take every bit as much work for classroom teachers as the most important lesson or unit. It will take preparation and planning, study and commitment. It takes a pedagogical model and practice. But it will be very worthwhile.

I hope that one day, one of the students whom I taught will receive a Nobel prize and declare his work to the glory of God—unlike the scientific naturalist who, when he won the Nobel prize for his work in the discovery of DNA, declared that the human is just a piece of junk.

I want my students to look at the mountains and the hills and declare something entirely different than the prayer of the religious humanist ("The world of stars, atoms, hill, trees [is] the source and final repository of my being"). I want my students to have a lifetime of worship directed toward God, the Creator, rather than toward the hills, His creation. Worldview beliefs matter!

I want my students to be good stewards of the earth. I want them to have a solid biblical view of care for the environment and an understanding of the relationships between living things, such as trees and humans and the exchanges of essential gases. But I do not want them worshiping or hugging an inflated globe. I do want them praising the Creator and proclaiming "this is my Father's world," and He has made it to be inhabited (Isaiah 45:18).

May God help us in the task of worldview integration, and may we encourage our young people toward integrative living as we accept the challenge and the hard work of planning and delivering a designed curriculum that is truly reflective of the Christian mind. May the result be seen in the lives of young people who will be thoroughly Christian in their thinking and acting in all areas of life *and* learning.

In comparing the worldviews of Freud and Lewis, Nicholi uses Gordon Allport's two categories of "religious" people: extrinsically and intrinsically religious people. Nicholi writes:

> Extrinsically religious people are those whose expressions of faith are motivated by a need to attain status or be accepted by others. Usually a child's faith, motivated by a need to please parents, falls into this category. Intrinsically religious people are those who internalize their beliefs so that they become the primary motivating influence in their lives.... [Extrinsic beliefs] are easily eroded by outside influences.

The goal of worldview integration in a Christian academic institution is to promote the internalization of a biblical worldview that will last a lifetime, not to promote "extrinsic beliefs" just to pass a course or please a teacher.

While I was cleaning out my files the other day, I found an old copy of the *Free Inquiry* magazine. One of the contributors to the Reader's Forum wrote that he had attended private school and received a fair amount of religious "indoctrination." But when he entered college he was confronted by "many belief systems, which showed me that the Judeo-Christian myth was just one of many ... I came to understand that human beings, not a deity, are the authors of goodness and evil ... The existence of the Christian deity was completely irrelevant to human experience." He went on to say that he came to the realization that, "life is a human adventure based on human values" (Condo 1989). He had come to a place where he, as a human, was the foundation for his worldview.

As I read these and other testimonials to lost faith, I was saddened. Christian school is not a place to indoctrinate to the point of protection from all other worldviews; nor is it a place to separate the "Bible" part from the "curriculum" part. It is place to study and learn together, to ask and answer questions, to be open and loving, and to guide our students toward informing their worldview by God's perspective revealed in His Word. We should be praying that God will transform their worldview (and ours, too) so that it will conform to God's view, that the end goal may be an *internalized,* biblically formed worldview out of which to think and act to the glory of God.

Walk the talk!

Appendix 1

Biblical Worldview Questions Adapted for Early Childhood

The following wrong thinking statements are provided as examples.

	Wrong Thinking: What Some People Say	Right Thinking: What the Bible Says
What is real?	"There is no God." "There may be some kind of an invisible force." "There is a God, but He really does not care about us or help us." "Only stuff you can touch is real."	God is real and He cares for every person. He is in charge of everything that happens on the earth He created. He made all else that is real, including us.
Where did everything that is alive or in nature come from?	"Everything that we see just sort of appeared or happened." "No one really knows."	God created all humans and all of nature. He created the earth to be lived in by humans and His created animals, fish, trees, flowers and other plants.
What is a human person?	"A person is just like any other animal, though maybe smarter." "A person is just bones and flesh."	A person is made to show much of what God is like. God says that we are made to be like Him. We not only have physical bodies, but also a spirit like God. We can think and learn, and we have feelings; we can make things and choose to do things.
What happens to people after they die?	"That's just the end of them. Their bodies are buried in the ground. It does not matter what they have believed or done in life."	The person lives on, either with God in heaven, or separated from God if the person has not asked Jesus to forgive his or her sins.
How do we decide what is right and wrong to think and do?	"People can decide for themselves what is right or wrong." "A group of people decides what is right for all in the group." "Nothing is wrong as long as no one gets hurt."	God tells us in the Bible what is right and wrong by helping us know what He is like. Jesus, His son who lived on earth, showed us God's character too. God's Holy Spirit helps us do what is right.

Why is it possible for us to learn and know things?	"We can only learn about the things we see, touch, hear, smell, taste—using our senses. Therefore we can't learn about God." "We can't really learn anything that is really true because we all think differently."	God created humans with the ability to learn using our minds and our senses, and He has provided something for us to learn—His world (all of creation) and His Word. He has let us know these things.
Why do we learn about how people lived and acted many years ago?	"There are popular stories about famous people, but we can't really know if they are true." "We can read about the past and learn how to do or not do things now." "The past is unimportant."	We can learn about God's perspective about all of life. We can see how He worked things out for people in the past and how He kept His promises. We can learn about people who loved and pleased God. History is important.
What does it mean to me to have answers to these big questions?	"These are my own beliefs and they will help me think about life. I decide what to believe all by myself."	I can decide to trust God and do what He says and live to please Him. Life will make sense as God intended it to be.

Questions adapted from *The Universe Next Door* by James Sire. Chart adapted from a chart created by Malinda Brown.

Appendix 2

Worldview Questions Answered by Theologians

What is prime reality? If it is God, what is His nature?

The starting point of a biblical worldview is an eternal, personal, and self-existent God (Genesis 1:1; John 1:1). The God of the Bible is eternal and complete in Himself. In the terms of classic theology, God is the ground of His own being; He needs no one else. He is described by His attributes—although He is more than the sum of His attributes. Each of His attributes is possessed infinitely. The attributes are complementary, never in conflict. In many ways, one needs to list the attributes to begin to describe the God of the Hebrew-Christian Scriptures. This God is personal and relational, for He is Trinity. He is completely separate from His creation (transcendent), yet able to relate personally with His creatures (immanent). At the same time but not in the same way, God is one and three. Each member of the Trinity possesses the same nature and characteristics—each, Father, Son and Holy Spirit, is fully God.

—Dr. Robert Kilgore — Trinity University

God, the Creator, is the ultimate reality. He is a relational God. There is a perfect relationship within the Trinity between the three persons of the Trinity; hence, they are described as one. The description of the three persons of the Trinity within Scripture is primarily functional and relational.

—Dr. John Master, ThD — Dallas Theological Seminary

The Scriptures do not attempt to prove the existence of God, but begin with His existence as the starting point of all that is. He is one in nature, and thus the only God. He is also revealed as three in persons: Father, Son, and Spirit. This has been termed the Trinity, or the triune God. This God is creator of all that exists. He is separate from His creation (transcendent), yet He relates to His creation (immanent). Immanence includes one member of the Trinity, the Son, taking on full humanity and living for a time within the creation. God has no limits except those inherent to His nature (e.g., He cannot sin). His characteristics have been listed in various ways, but the clearest way to know about God is through what He has revealed of Himself in His word.

—Dr. Gordon Gregory, University of South Africa

What is the nature of external reality, that is, the world (cosmos, universe) around us?

Reality includes the entire universe, including space itself. The universe and all that is in it was created directly by God's power, expressed through His spoken Word. We conclude that all that exists is directly from God, and planned for His glory and the wellbeing of the humans He made after His own image and likeness. In many places, the Bible affirms that God created and sustains the universe (Genesis 1–2; Isaiah 45:18; John 1:1–4; Colossians 1:16–17; Hebrews 1:2–3).

—Dr. Robert Kilgore — Trinity University

The external reality was created by God. It is sustained by divine power. According to Genesis 1–2 the primary function of the external world is to provide a suitable habitat for humankind.

—Dr. John Master, ThD — Dallas Theological Seminary

God created all that we see—all that is not God. He also sustains the universe through His power. It would cease to exist without His hand maintaining it. The world as we know it today is not as God created it because it has been corrupted through sin. This corruption affects every aspect of creation, including humanity.

—Dr. Gordon Gregory, University of South Africa

What or who is a human being?

Humans are conscious beings formed after the image and likeness of God, designed to reflect God's glory on earth. The creation of Adam and Eve must be viewed as having two distinct origins: the physical body was created out of the dust of the ground (Genesis 2:7) but the immaterial nature was created directly by the breath of God, an expression of God's power and nature. Adam and Eve were created holy. That holiness was not absolute as is God's holiness; it was untested holiness. God placed a single test in the Garden, the prohibition to eat of the tree of the knowledge of good and evil. Adam and Eve failed the test, she by deception and he deliberately. The result is that sin entered the world, along with death, corruption of the human nature, and all kinds of evil. The most devastating result of sin is that apart from Christ, humans remain separated from God.

—Dr. Robert Kilgore, Trinity University

Human beings are a unique part of the Genesis 1–2 creation and stand between God and the rest of His creation uniquely by virtue of the fact that humankind is made out of the earth (creation) yet related to God by being made in God's image.

—Dr. John Master, ThD, Dallas Theological Seminary

The most basic fact about humans is that we are created in God's image, which entails being created to have a relationship with God, display His glory, and have dominion over the rest of creation. Our relationship with God has been severed—we do not display God's glory as intended—and the domain of humanity's dominion has been subject to futility. The image and its entailments can only be restored through God's gracious redemption in Christ. Adam was originally created from the dust (related to the creation), but his life came from God's breath (related to God); we are a complex unity of material and immaterial.

—Dr. Gordon Gregory, University of South Africa

Is there life after death? What happens to a person at death?

God created humans to experience eternal fellowship with Him. Sin broke that fellowship, and humans became separated from God. That fellowship is restored in Christ so that by faith people can enjoy fellowship with God forever. Sin did not change the immortal nature of humanity so that those who do not express faith in God will spend an eternity separated from God.

—*Dr. Robert Kilgore, Trinity University*

At death, the invisible "part" of man is separated from the visible "part" of man. The creation of Adam out of the dust of the earth and receiving the breath of lives (lit. plural) reflects the visible and invisible nature of humanity. The visible/invisible distinction is from the perspective of those living on earth. What, at the present, is invisible to us will be visible when we die.

—*Dr. John Master, ThD, Dallas Theological Seminary*

Because of sin, death entered the world. For the believer in Christ, death leads to a separation of body and soul, with the soul immediately going to be with Christ. At the return of Christ, all people will be resurrected: believers to eternal life in the New Jerusalem in God's presence forever; and unbelievers to eternal condemnation in the lake of fire, separated from God forever.

—*Dr. Gordon Gregory, University of South Africa*

Why is it possible to know at all? How do we come to know?

God can be known through His self-disclosure. Apart from God's sovereign initiative, it would not be possible to know Him (1 Corinthians 2:10–12). God is unknowable (Job 11:7; Isaiah 40:18) and at the same time knowable (John 14:7; 17:3; 1 John 5:20). Both are true in a non-absolute way. He can be known but cannot be fully known.

—*Dr. Robert Kilgore, Trinity University*

God made us as relational beings. To have relationships we must have knowledge. God gave us this ability. We come to know through our experiences and through God's revelation.

—*Dr. John Master, ThD, Dallas Theological Seminary*

Just as God has intellect, so humans created in God's image have intellect, and thus the ability to know. Just as God perceives, so humans created in God's image have organs of perception. While God perceives all reality directly, our organs of perception (senses) give us the ability to gather data from the world around us. Beyond the ability to gather information through our senses, God has also given humans revelation in various forms to know Him and His will.

—*Dr. Gordon Gregory, University of South Africa*

What is the basis for morality? How do we know what is right and wrong?

God Himself is the standard of right and wrong. He reflects perfection in nature, thought, and action. God's will for our moral response in recorded in His Word, the Bible. His will is embedded in direct commands, "you shall not steal" (Exodus 20:15b), and "You shall love the Lord your God with all your heart and with all your soul and with all your strength and with all your mind, and your neighbor as yourself" (Luke 10:27 ESV). His will is also embedded in principles throughout Scripture (e.g. the narratives of the Old Testament and the parables of the Gospels). Ultimately we know right and wrong by knowing God, the source of all ethics.

—Dr. Robert Kilgore, Trinity University

Right and wrong only have meaning if there is a standard that is universal; otherwise, right and wrong are merely opinions. The standard is God's character, revealed in His Word.

—Dr. John Master, ThD, Dallas Theological Seminary

God determines morality, not because He says something is right or wrong, but because He is righteous and whatever aligns with His character is right. Conversely, anything that does not accord with His character is wrong. We also speak of God's will determining right and wrong, but His will always conforms to His character. We know right and wrong ultimately from God revealing it to us.

—Dr. Gordon Gregory, University of South Africa

What is the meaning of human history?

History may appear to repeat itself, but history is moving toward God demonstrating victory over sin, Satan, and human sinfulness. Human history has movements: creation, fall, God demonstrating blessing for obedience and suffering as the result of disobedience to His will (basically the Old Testament), God demonstrating His love and grace in the incarnation of Christ, God displaying His glory through followers of Christ (the rest of the New Testament and the age of the church), and God displaying His glory through Christ reigning on earth.

—Dr. Robert Kilgore, Trinity University

Human history is a revelation of God's grace. History is, after all, "His story."

—Dr. John Master, ThD , Dallas Theological Seminary

Human history's ultimate purpose is the ultimate purpose of all things: to glorify God. God is sovereign over history and His purposes will prevail. History's center is the incarnation of Christ and the work accomplished by Him in His death, resurrection, and ascension. It is moving inexorably toward the return of Christ, the subduing of all things under the authority of Christ, the righteous judgment of God, and the establishment of the new heaven and new earth. What God intended for all creation, and particularly for humanity, will be accomplished.

—Dr. Gordon Gregory, University of South Africa

What are the personal life core commitments consistent with one's worldview? What are the implications of my beliefs for life (and learning)?

Belief in the God who has revealed Himself in the Scriptures means we give willing obedience to God and His revealed will, which leads us to worship God for who He is and to reflect the character of the God who has spoken to the world He created.

—Dr. Robert Kilgore, Trinity University

Jesus said that without Him we can do nothing. Recognizing the gift of God's grace is the critical factor that should mark out a believer. Since every gift comes from above, we should recognize our responsibility to our creator and use His gifts wisely for His glory.

—Dr. John Master, ThD, Dallas Theological Seminary

In light of all that has been said above, the most important commitment to make is aligning one's life with God's purposes. That includes having a relationship with God through faith in the work of Christ in His death and resurrection; becoming more conformed to the image of Christ each day; making disciples according to Christ's commission; taking part in the dominion God gave to humans at creation; and looking for and working towards Christ's return.

—Dr. Gordon Gregory, University of South Africa

Appendix 3

Cognitive Interactive Teaching Model

Bible Lesson Illustration: Life of Joseph (Genesis 39–50)

Target/Focus (Big Idea): God is in control of our personal life circumstances/history. He can use the good and the bad events for our good and His good purposes. We can trust Him.

Response Aim: The student will trust God to work all things in his life for good.

Instructional Objective: The student will be able to explain and defend God's good work in all of life's circumstances using the life of Joseph.

1. **Motivation—engage the mind** of the student and activate the mind toward the *truth to be learned.*

   Method: *PowerPoint slide activity:* flour, sugar, chocolate chips, etc. (cookie ingredients)

   Each student decides whether or not he/she likes the taste of each as a separate item. **Caution:** Be aware of students' food allergies, such as nuts, gluten, etc. Do not let students consume raw eggs.

   Each student will count the number of ingredients he/she likes as a single spoon full. Share number with class.

   Teacher asks: When put together, what do you think these ingredients might become? (chocolate chip cookies) How is it that some things that taste bad by themselves can become a delicious cookie? What is the process needed? (a person who knows the recipe, right amount of each ingredient, how hot to heat the oven, how long to leave the cookies in, etc.)

   Bridge to new information: The life of Joseph is in some ways like the cookie and the ingredients. Let's see if we can find out how. As you work on your study of Joseph's life today, ask yourself, "How is Joseph's life like the chocolate chip cookie?

2. **New Information Getting** (Concept Development)—New information into a ready mind. For this lesson, the content is biblical and it must be processed and learned by the student.

   Method: Inductive study of the life of Joseph (Genesis 37–50)—Teacher creates a chart; students read and summarize the passages and determine if each event was a good (+) or bad (-) event.

   Guiding Questions: How did Joseph view the bad events in his life? How do you know? What Scripture verse is evidence for your answer? Be able to defend your answer.

Joseph's Life		
Genesis Reference	Description of the passage	Good (+) or bad (-)?
37:2–10, 19		
37:21, 22		
37:25–28		
39:1–6		
39:6–20		
40:1–5		
40:23		
41:1		
41:9–14		
41:41		

3. Student Processing Activities: Process, relate, and categorize information. Draw conclusions or state generalizations—truth to be *internalized and connected* to students' lives so that they can understand, store, and use the new information and respond to God.

Methods: Let's go back to our cookie ingredients:
- What did the life of Joseph have in common with the ingredients and final product of the cookies?
- What verse in the text shows that Joseph knew the outcome was good? (Genesis 50:20)
- Make a list of one or two good things God has brought into your life this year.
- Make a list of any not-so-good things allowed in your life this year. How is your list different from Joseph's? Similar?

Whiteboard/chalkboard or PowerPoint slide activity:
List the good and bad things in Joseph's life and compare them to the student's life.

Good	*Bad*
Joseph: Loved by his father	Joseph: Hated by brothers
Students: Love of friends and family	Students: Not liked by classmates or family member
Joseph: Made a leader in prison and in Potiphar's house	Joseph: Butler promised but didn't follow through
Students: School, community, and church leadership roles.	Student: Someone promised but did not do what was promised

If we view our circumstances as Joseph did, what might we say about our own good and bad events? Write one thing in your journal or share it with a friend.

Pairs: Activity to help one another remember this hard truth. Decide one way to help remember, e.g. memorize Romans 8:28–29. Decide on other ways to hold each other accountable.

Music: There are several songs which set Romans 8:28 to music. I have used "All Things Work Together for Good" in my lessons.

4. **Assessing learning:** Concept (big idea) drawn out for *use* in a new (but familiar to students) authentic situation.

When Joseph said to his brothers, "You meant it unto me as harm but God meant it for our good," what did Joseph mean? Explain what he meant in your own words and particularly use the part "harm *me*" and "*our* good."

Situation Activity: A Christian friend is going through some difficulty with a family member, or perhaps has experienced cyber-bullying. Use ideas from the life of Joseph (references) and the truth learned to encourage him/her. Share what you might say with a partner. Or write a text message, e-mail, or letter to him or her. Let the students select the format. This is feedback to assess whether students are "getting it."

Cognitive Interactive Model:

1. Goes well beyond the learning of discrete facts such as names, places, and events. It takes the student beyond the memorized generalization of the content as well. However, content knowledge is vital!

2. Focuses the mind toward the information to be learned from the start so that the information (in this case, Bible content) begins to be put into a meaningful framework for understanding.

3. It helps the student *relate* the content to his own experiences and therefore uses conceptual categories or prior knowledge or experiences already in the mind and life of the student.

4. It provides opportunity for the student to mentally manipulate the information and use it in a situation close to his/her life.

5. It provides feedback to the teacher and the student that indicates understanding or lack of understanding.

This model is used for all subject areas because it is developed out of human learning theory. However, the methods used for each element will vary with grade level and subject matter.

Appendix 4

"Big Ideas" by Subject Area

Sample Work on Answering Worldview Questions

These are additional issues related to the eight key worldview questions found in *The Universe Next Door*. These particular questions were identified by a senior class of teacher education majors at Cairn University. The 35 students were grouped according to subject area (secondary teaching students by their certification area and elementary education majors by the subject area of their choice).

Fine Arts and Performing Arts

God created music and art to be used for His glory and to praise Him (Psalm 150).

God gave man the capacity and desire to respond to God and creation through art and music.

Since man exists to glorify God, his art and music should also exist for that purpose.

Man has a responsibility to develop his God-given talents of art and music to their fullest extent.

Music and art are amoral avenues for moral communication.

Humankind, created in God's image, express themselves (thinking and feelings) through the arts. (1 Corinthians 14:15, "I will sing with my spirit, but I will also sing with my understanding."

Music and art reflect transcendent reality.

- God, a transcendent being, gives meaning to artistic expression.
- Some qualities of God are revealed in the creative order inherent to music and art.

Music and art reflect human beings created in the image of God, the creative one.

- Something of the character of God is revealed in the reflection of created human beings.
- Though not untainted by the sinful nature of humankind, music and art do exemplify the creative and expressive qualities possessed by all those created in God's image.

Art and music are the expressions of human thinking (worldviews and feelings).

Music and art have a context within history.

- Evidence a progression within the larger scope of human history and thought.
- Display a given philosophical and moral purpose or presuppositions.

Music is an eternal activity, a Scripture-appointed means to frame the praises of God both for the present and the future. (Music is in heaven as well as on earth.)

Math/Science

God communicates quantitatively and has given humans the minds to do so as well.

God gives us the ability to think spatially and numerically to better understand our universe and to communicate with one another.

The logic applied to mathematics helps give evidence for the existence of God (truths, axioms). God exists. He is ultimate reality (Genesis 1:1, Psalm 90:2). He is "self-evident".

He is creator and spoke the world into existence (Genesis 1). He is sustainer of the universe.

He sustains His creation.

He is omnipotent (seen through creation, Genesis 1, Psalm 139, Colossians 1, John 1, Romans 1).

God is infinite.

He is intelligent and a God of design.

Man is a special creation of God; we are created in His image (Psalm 139).

Humans have not evolved from impersonal material (Genesis 1).

Humans are intelligent, qualitatively different from the animal kingdom.

We know many things through the scientific method (sensory experience and reason).

God has chosen to disclose Himself in nature—His power and His godhead.

God is a God of order.

The body is the temple of God. Man is responsible for the care of the body. Physical exercise is important for good health. We need to take care of and use our bodies to bring glory to God in our life.

God has sustained man throughout human history. The purpose for man is to glorify God. God has allowed man to use his abilities to invent, search, discover, and learn. As humans use the senses correctly, God is glorified and humans are sustained with life.

There is order in the universe. God created the earth with order and regularity to be inhabited.

Through God's revelation, we can see that God is rational and logical.

Through God's Word, we can see God uses number and quantity as a way of communication.

As Fibonacci discovered, God uses sequential mathematics in nature.

Through His creation (humans, plants, animals), we see God's use of symmetry.

God uses numbers in conventional ways. ("Be fruitful and multiply," 70 x 7 = 490 yrs., tithe 1/10 of earnings.)

Language Arts

God is a communicator. Humans are created in God's image and are, therefore, communicators by nature.

God communicated with humankind through spoken word, written word, and His creation. We can speak to Him and others and read His word and the words of others.

The human is a rational being able to think and communicate his thoughts and feelings.

Humankind's ability to communicate thoughts and feelings is demonstrated in the writing of books and articles, and in human interaction.

The way of knowing by revelation is found in God's Word. Therefore if there is clear conflict between man's thoughts and God's thoughts, His Word sits in judgment (Exodus 4:10–11).

God is responsible not only for speech (use of auditory and graphic symbols), but for the creation of different languages (Genesis 11:7–9).

What kind of God is He?

- God is a communicating God.
- He is creative and inventive.

What or who is man?

- Made in the image of God, so therefore he is a communicator, thinker, writer, speaker, and maker. He is relational, emotional, curious, and creative by nature.

How do we know?

- God has created humans with the capacity to know and learn. There are many ways to know: written revelation, history, observation, recorded writings, etc. The language arts are vital in learning.

God has allowed humans to grow in knowledge and "be able to come to the knowledge of truth" because He has given His word as a lens through which all else can be viewed.

God gave us the ability to effectively communicate with Him and with each other.

Various worldviews are seen in literature, but we know that God's character is the standard for right and wrong and for answering the basic questions of life often dealt with in literature.

Man is created in the image of God, although fallen, and is to glorify God. We have purpose. Literature often questions who the human is and addresses the search for meaning in human history.

Because humankind is made in the image of God and is rational, he can read, write, listen, talk, and reason.

The Bible itself contains various genre of literature, such as poetry, parables, history, and narratives.

Social Studies

Humankind is special—created in the image of God. He is sinful by nature; therefore, problems occur in all areas of human endeavor studied by the social sciences.

Man is a moral being and is responsible to act according to God's standards.

God is in ultimate control of all history.

God is omniscient.

God uses history to teach us.

History is the outworking of God's plan for humankind.

Man is a relational/social being—by nature—created in God's image.

Man is in need of redemption.

Man has a delegated sovereignty over creation (under God).

God is at work in history. History is "his story" (a narrative of...)

God is in control of raising up leaders and putting them down as He purposes.

Morality is based on God's character.

Key Questions:

What or who is man?

What is God's purpose for historical events? Why does He allow war? Why is there evil in the world?

Is God sovereign? Who is in control?

Does man need interaction?

Why am I where I am and as I am? (culture)

Should Christians be involved in politics?

Should we obey authorities?
- When we disagree with authority?
- When the authority disagrees with God's Word?

Why did God create the family?
- What is the purpose?

Why am I in this family? What is the purpose for government?

Who is the head of the family?

Should we pray for leaders in the government?

Did God specifically "organize" the earth this way?

Where did man originate?

Why did God create a will and emotions? What makes a human have personhood?

How can emotions/will be used in society?

What is a human's purpose in society?

How can you carry out the purpose in society?

Is there life after death?

What is the difference between biblical principles and "cultural traditions"?

What is the basis for morality?

How should we treat others?

Who supplies our needs?

- How should we use what God gives us?

Why did God create us unique and different from each other? In what ways can we see this? Why should we have a global perspective?

Physical Education

Physical education takes into consideration the whole person. The education of the physical is for the development of the body, mind, and emotions. It is a discipline of both mind and body. Physical education touches all parts of life (mental, physical, social, emotional...)

We are responsible for healthy treatment of our bodies (1 Corinthians 6:19–20).

Teamwork in the church is a biblical mandate (Romans 12:4).

God is concerned with the body He gave us and what we do with it. Physical and spiritual are interrelated in our care for our bodies and our human sexuality (1 Thessalonians 4:4)

For the sake of the gospel, Paul disciplined his physical body (1 Corinthians 9:23–27).

Self-discipline speaks to, or about, spiritual disciplines.

Science/Health

God is a God of order (1 Corinthians 14:33).

God is the Creator (Genesis 1:1).

God sustains all things (Hebrews 1:3).

The heavens declare the glory of God (Psalms 19:1–2).

We come to know, in part, through general revelation.

All human beings die.

Human beings have design.

Through creation we can know some of God's goodness.

God's purposes are fulfilled through a sequence of events.

God's attributes are shown in death, life, and sustaining of life.

Works Cited

Adler, J. 2006. "The New Naysayers." *Newsweek*. Retrieved from *http://www.newsweek.com/new-naysayers-109697*

Adler, M. 1985. *Ten philosophical mistakes*. New York: MacMillan Publishing Company.

American Heritage Dictionary of English Language, 5th Ed. 2011. Boston: Houghton Mifflin Harcourt Publishing Company.

Beane, J. Ed. 1995. *Toward a coherent curriculum*. The 1995 ASCD Yearbook. Alexandria, VA: Association of Supervision and Curriculum Development.

Berenstain, J. and S. Berenstain. 1997. *The Berenstain bears' big book of science and nature*. New York: Random House.

Bigge, M. and S. Shermis. 2004. *Learning theories for teachers*. Boston: Allyn & Bacon, Pearson Education, Inc.

Bloom, A. 1987. *The closing of the American mind*. New York: Simon and Schuster.

Bruner, J. 1977. *The process of education*. Cambridge, MA: Harvard University Press. Original work published in 1960.

Camus, A. 1961. *Resistance, rebellion and death*. New York: Alfred A Knopf, Inc.

Capra, F. 1985. *The tao of physics: An exploration of the parallels between modern physics and eastern mysticism*, 2nd Ed. London: Bantam Press Division of Random House.

Carter, S. 1993. *Culture of disbelief: How American law and politics trivialize religious devotion*. New York: Basic Books, Division of Harper Collins.

Chopra, D. 1992. *Escaping the prison of the mind: A journey from here to here*. San Rafael, CA: New World Library, audiocassette book.

Chopra, D. 2014. "Five Spiritual Mysteries: #1 Is Karma Fair? [Part 2]" *Chopra Foundation News,* Retrieved from http://www.choprafoundation.org.

Chopra, D. 2014. "Our Future Depends on Spirituality and Science Working Together." Retrieved May 2014 from the huffingtonpost.com/Deepak-chopra.

Chubb, J. and T. Moe. 1990. *Politics, markets, and America's schools*. Washington, D.C.: The Brookings Institute.

Clark, G. 1981. *A Christian view of men and things*. Grand Rapids: Baker Book House.

Collins English Dictionary—Complete & Unabridged. 2012. Digital Edition © William Collins Sons & Co. Ltd. 1979, 1986 © HarperCollins Publishers

Condo, F. 1989. "Growing Toward Unbelief," *Free Inquiry*, Vol.9, No.4. Buffalo, NY: Council for Democratic and Secular Humanism.

Corduan, W. 1993. *Reasonable faith: Basic Christian apologetics*. Nashville: Broadman and Holman Publishers.

Costa, A. 2008. "Teaching Students to Think." *Educational Leadership, February* 2008 | Volume 65 | Number 5. Alexandria, VA: Association of Supervision and Curriculum Development.

Cott, J. and C. Doudna. 1982. Lennon, Sean in *The Ballad of John and Yoko*. Rolling Stone Press. Retrieved from http://www.johnlennon.talktalk.net/lennon.html.

Dawkins, R. 1998. *River out of Eden*. United Kingdom: Phoenix.

Dawkins, R. 2006. *The god delusion*. Great Britain: Bantam Press.

Deitrick Price, B. 2015. "Critical Thinking—if only." #59. Improve Education.org. Retrieved April 2015 from http://www.improve-education.org/id87.html.

Dennett, D. 2006. *Breaking the spell*. New York: Penguin Books.

Dunkel, H. 1969. *Herbart and education*. New York: Random House.

Froebel, F. in Weber, E. 1969. *The kindergarten*. New York: Teachers College Press.

von Glasersfeld, E. 1995. *Radical constructivism: a way of knowing and learning*. Washington, D.C.: The Falmer Press.

Greene, A. 1977. Pages from A Euro-Notebook. *Vanguard,* May/June 1977.

Goleman, D. 1987. "Embattled giant of psychology speaks his mind." *New York Times*, August 25. 1987.

Hart, H., J. van der Hoeven, N. Wolterstorff. 1983. *Rationality in the Calvin tradition*. Toronto: University Press of America.

Hitchens, C. 2007. *God is not great: the case against religion.* London: Atlantic Books

Huffman, D. Ed. 2011. *Christian contours: How a biblical worldview shapes the mind and heart.* Grand Rapids: Kregel Publications.

Humanist Manifesto I. 1933. *The New Humanist* VI:3:1-5 May/June 1933

Humanist Manifesto II. 1973. Retrieved from *http://americanhumanist.org/Humanism/Humanist_Manifesto_II*

Humanist Manifesto III. 2003. Retrieved from *http://americanhumanist.org/Humanism/Humanist_Manifesto_II*

Huxley, A. 1937. *Ends and means: An inquiry into the nature of ideals.* London, Great Britain: Oxford University Press. Retrieved from http://www.archive.org/stream/endsandmeans035237mbp/endsandmeans035237mbp_djvu.txt

Jeffers, S. 2002. *Brother eagle, sister sky: The words of chief Seattle.* New York, NY. Penquin Books. words retrieved January 2015 from arvindguptatoys.com/arvindgupta/chiefseattle.pdf

Johnson, C. *The Earth is my mother*, retrieved April 2015 from http://www.songsforteaching.com/caroljohnson/theearthismymother.htm.

Jacobs, A. J. 2007. *The year of living biblically.* New York: Simon and Schuster.

Klassen, H. 2010. *Visual valet.* Kandern Germany: Teach Beyond Publishing.

Knight, G. 2006. *Philosophy in education: An introduction in Christian perspective.* Berrien Springs, MI: Andrews University Press.

Kurtz, P. 2000. *Humanist manifesto 2000: A call for planetary humanism.* Amherst, NY: Prometheus Books.

Kuyper, A, tr. George Kamps. 1880. "Sphere Sovereignty." Retrieved from Reformation Publishing Project: http://reformationalpublishingproject.com/pdf_books/Scanned_Books_PDF/SphereSovereignty_English.pdf.

LeBar, L. 1958. *Education that is Christian.* Old Tappan, NJ: Fleming H. Revell Company.

Lewis, C.S. 1952. *Mere Christianity.* New York: HarperOne.

MacLaine, S. 1985. *Dancing in the light.* New York: Bantam Books.

Martel, Y. 2001. *The life of Pi.* New York: Harcourt, Inc.

Mohler Jr., A. 2005. "Moralistic Therapeutic Deism." *The Christian Post,* April 18, 2005 retrieved from, http://www.christianpost.com/news/6266/#ILoFSEwquTsFolLX.99

Mohler, A. 2010. "The Christian Worldview as Master Narrative." December 15, 2010. Retrieved from http://www.albertmohler.com/2011/01/10/the-christian-worldview-as-master-narrative-redemption-accomplished/

Mondale, L. 1996. The Lingering Humanist Manifesto I. *Free Inquiry.* Vol 16. Buffalo, NY: Council for Democratic and Secular Humanism

Moreland, J.P. 2007. *Kingdom triangle: Recover the Christian mind, renovate the soul, restore the Spirit's power.* Grand Rapids, MI: Zondervan.

Newberger Goldstein, R. 2014. "How Philosophy Makes Progress." *The Chronicle of Higher Education: The Chronicle Review.* Retrieved from http://chronicle.com/article/Is-Philosophy-Obsolete-/145837/

Nicholi Jr., A. 2002. *The question of God.* New York: The Free Press.

Nixon, R. January 29, 1969. First inaugural address as President of the USA. Retrieved from Yale Law School, Lillian Goldman Law Library http://avalon.law.yale.edu/20th_century/nixon1.asp

Nizkor Project. 1946. The Trial of German Major War Criminals, Nuremberg, Germany. Retrieved from http://www.nizkor.org/hweb/imt/tgmwc/tgmwc-19/tgmwc-19-188-04.shtml First published Under the Authority of H.M. Attorney-General By His Majesty's Stationery Office, London.

Oaklander, M. 2015. "The Art of Resilience." *Time* Vol.185, No.20. Time, Inc: New York.

Olsen, T. 2002. "Buffy's Religion." *Christianity Today.* July 8, 2002. Retrieved from http://www.christianitytoday.com/ct/2002/.html

Osborne, J. 1957. *The entertainer.* London: Faber and Faber.

Pearcey, N. 2010. *Saving Leonardo.* Nashville, TN: B&H Publishing.

Plantinga Jr., C. 2002. *Engaging God's world: A Christian vision of faith, learning, and living.* Grand Rapids: Eerdmans Publishing Company.

Prothero, S. 2010. *God is not one.* New York: HarperCollins.

Ryken, L. 1986. *Culture and Christian perspective.* Portland, OR: Multnomah Press

Sartre, J. 1948. tr. Philip Mairet. *Existentialism and humanism.* London: Methuen.

Sarte, J. and W. Baskins Ed. 1993. *Essays in existentialism.* New York: Citadel Press

Schaeffer, F. 1968. *The God who is there.* Chicago: Inter-Varsity Press.

Schaeffer, F. 1981, 2005. A *Christian manifesto.* Wheaton, IL: Crossway Books.

Schlossberg, H. 1983. *Idols for destruction.* Nashville, TN: Thomas Nelson Publishers

Scriven, M. and R. Paul. 1987. A statement by Michael Scriven and Richard Paul, 8th Annual International Conference on Critical Thinking and Education Reform, summer 1987. Retrieved from The Critical Thinking Community http://www.criticalthinking.org/pages/defining-critical-thinking/766

Sellars, R. 1933. Religious Humanism, *The New Humanist* May-June, 1933. VI: 3:7-12. Chicago: American Humanist Association

Sire, J. 2004. *Naming the elephant: worldview as a concept.* Downer's Grove, IL.: Inter Varsity Press

Sire, J. 2009. *The universe next door.* 5th Edition. Downer's Grove, IL.: Inter Varsity Press

Social Science Staff of the Educational Research Council of America. 1971. *Four world views: the human adventure.* Boston: Allyn and Bacon, Inc.

Solomon, R. 1974. *Existentialism.* New York: McGraw-Hill.

Solzhenitsyn, A. 1978. "A World Split Apart." Address at Harvard on June 8, 1978. Retrieved from Orthodoxy Today.com http://www.orthodoxytoday.org/articles/SolzhenitsynHarvard.php

Spencer, H. 1860, 1909. *Education: intellectual, moral and physical.* New York: D Appleton & Company.

Stedman, C. 2014. "Nick Sagan on 'Cosmos,' Carl, and his 'strange childhood,'" *Religion News Service.* Mar 16, 2014 | Retrieved from http://chrisstedman.religionnews.com/2014/03/16/cosmos-nick-sagan-strange-childhood/#sthash.itoctu81.dpuf

Steinem, G. 1992. *Revolution from within: a book of self esteem.* New York: Little, Brown, and Company.

Sternberg, R. 2001. "Schools Should Teach for Wisdom: The Balance Theory of Wisdom in Educational Settings." *Educational Psychologist* 36 4, 227–245. Hillsdale, NJ: Lawrence Erlbaum Associates

Sternberg, R. 2003. *Wisdom, intelligence, and creativity synthesized.* New York: Cambridge University Press.

Sumner, W. G. 1940. *Folkways: A study of the sociological importance of usages, manners, customs, mores, and morals.* New York: Ginn and Co.

Swartz, R. 1986. "Restructuring curriculum for critical thinking." *Educational Leadership.* Alexandria, VA: Association for Supervision and Curriculum Development.

Taylor, J., R. Eve, and F. Harrold. 1995. "Why Creationists Don't Go to Psychic Fairs." *Skeptical Inquirer.* November/December Issue.

Thomas, A. and G. Thorne. 2009. "How to increase higher level thinking." Metarie, LA: Center for Development and Learning. http://www.readingrockets.org/article/34655

Waltham, D. 2014. "Alone in the Universe." *Chronicle of Higher Education,* April 2014.

Wilkens, S. and M. Standford. 2009. *Hidden worldviews.* Downer's Grove, IL: InterVarsity Press.

Wolters, A. 2005. *Creation regained: Biblical basis for a reformational worldview,* 2nd Ed. Grand Rapids: Wm. B. Eerdmans Publishing Company.

World Pantheism Statement of Principles. *World pantheism official website*: Retrieved February 2015 http://www.pantheism.net/manifest.htm

Zacharias, R. 1996. *Deliver us from evil: Restoring the soul in a disintegrating culture.* Dallas, TX: Word Publishing.

Zacharias, R. 2000. *Jesus among other gods.* Nashville, TN: Word Publishing a Thomas Nelson Company

Zahorik, J. 1995. "Constructivist Teaching." *Phi Delta Kappa Fastback* 390. Bloomington, IN: Phi Delta Kappa Educational Foundation.